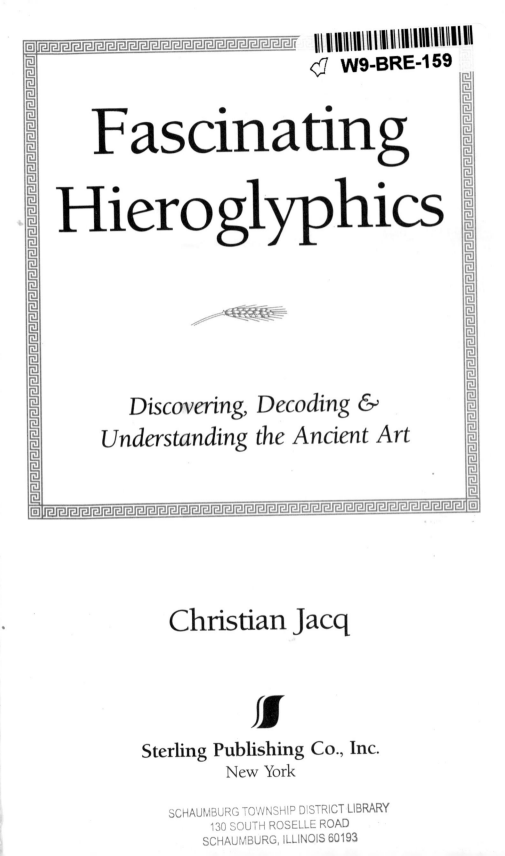

Fascinating Hieroglyphics

Discovering, Decoding &
Understanding the Ancient Art

Christian Jacq

Sterling Publishing Co., Inc.
New York

Translated by Catherine Berthier

Library of Congress Cataloging-in-Publication Data

Jacq, Christian.
    [Petit Champollion illustré. English]
    Fascinating hieroglyphics : discovering, decoding, and under-
standing the ancient art / Christian Jacq.
        p.   cm.
    Includes indexes.
    ISBN 0-8069-8100-8
    1. Egyptian language—Writing, Hieroglyphic.   I. Title.
PJ1097.J2713 1996
493'.1—dc20   96–29205
                                                                    CIP

10 9 8 7 6 5 4 3 2

First paperback edition published in 1998 by
Sterling Publishing Company, Inc.
387 Park Avenue South, New York, N.Y. 10016
Originally published in France © 1994 by Éditions Robert Laffont S.A.,
Paris under the title *Le petit Champollion illustré*
The MacHieroglyphics™ fonts used to print this work are © 1991–1995
by the Payne-Loving Trust and are available from Linguist's Software, Inc.
P.O. Box 580, Edmonds, WA 9802-0580
English translation © 1997 by Sterling Publishing Company, Inc.
Distributed in Canada by Sterling Publishing
% Canadian Manda Group, One Atlantic Avenue, Suite 105
Toronto, Ontario, Canada M6K 3E7
Distributed in Great Britain and Europe by Cassell PLC
Wellington House, 125 Strand, London WC2R 0BB, England
Distributed in Australia by Capricorn Link (Australia) Pty Ltd.
P.O. Box 6651, Baulkham Hills, Business Centre, NSW 2153, Australia
Manufactured in the United States of America
All rights reserved

Sterling ISBN 0-8069-8100-8 Trade
            0-8069-8699-9 Paper

Contents

Introduction

A French Egyptologist by the name of Rougé at one time wrote: "Once the hieroglyphic duck bites, it doesn't let go."

And it is true that this duck, which is used to write the word "son," is a tenacious fowl over five thousand years young, whose bite keeps the love of ancient Egypt alive in the heart and mind of its victims. To say that you have been bitten by the duck (or bug) of hieroglyphs means that you are truly passionate.

Fifty years ago, only a few scholars were interested in the language of ancient Egypt, and that passion often had them labeled "odd." Things have certainly changed since. It is now possible to read and write in hieroglyphs in many countries, be it in university or private lessons, and many amateurs are trying to decipher hieroglyphic texts and relive the adventures Jean François Champollion, the Frenchman who founded Egyptology.

This small book does not pretend to turn you into a committed Egyptologist, nor does it enable you to read a papyrus as if it were a newspaper, but it can initiate you into the spirit of hieroglyphs and invite you to take a few steps into this fascinating universe.

It takes years of study to read hieroglyphs correctly and decipher difficult texts—some of which still retain their secrets and pose problems.

But it is possible to understand "how it works" and

share the ancient Egyptians' view of the world. They were, after all, the creators of a civilization that we may well consider the mother of our culture. What could be more refreshing than a stroll among the hieroglyphs when these signs begin speaking to us? Don't worry—you won't find here an in-depth grammatical study; our purpose is much more modest. What we want to do is present some basic elements in an accessible manner, thus enabling you to identify some basic hieroglyphs. One of our most important aids will be the drawings, since you have to look at hieroglyphs before reading them.

With a bit of practice, you can become familiar with the duck and its fellow creatures. In this book, I sometimes express an idea first in hieroglyphs, and then in English, and I must say that I usually find the hieroglyphics superior. After all, doesn't having the idea, the image, and the sound in a single sign mean that you have a complete language at your disposal?

The civilization of ancient Egypt was one in which joy dominated. This small book's only pretension is to let its readers have, to use an ancient Egyptian expression, "hieroglyphs in the nose," which means that you enjoy and get pleasure from them.

Part One

FACE TO FACE WITH HIEROGLYPHS

1 The Deciphering Epic

I LOST MY HIEROGLYPHS, OR THE ANGUISH OF CHAMPOLLION

Before approaching the duck more closely, let's go to Egypt—more precisely to the town of Rosetta, in August 1799. It is there that Bouchard, a brilliant officer in General Bonaparte's Expeditionary Corps, first pulled out of the ground a stone covered with inscriptions. The valiant soldier was unable to decipher the text, which was in fact a decree framed by priests to honor King Ptolemy V in 196 B.C. When called upon, experts realized that three ancient languages were in use on the stone: Greek, Demotic (a language used towards the end of ancient Egyptian civilization), and hieroglyphs.

A tempting hypothesis was quickly formed: was this the same text, in three different languages? In other words, were we finally in possession of a Greek translation of a hieroglyphic text that would, after fourteen centuries of silence and mystery, allow us to understand this ancient language?

Hieroglyphs had become a mute language with the 7th century A.D. conquest of Egypt by the Arabs. No one knew how to read these strange symbols. Some called them magical; the ancients said that they held the secrets of priests.

During the 1st century A.D., Philon the Jew wrote:

Egyptian discourse constitutes a philosophy that is expressed by means of symbols, a philosophy that is revealed by letters which they term "sacred."

The philosopher Plotinus went even further when he wrote during the 3rd century A.D.:

Egyptian sages showed their consummate science by using symbolic signs, which, in a sense, they were able to designate intuitively without using the spoken word . . . Thus, each hiero-glyph constituted a sort of science or wisdom.

These are not trivial opinions, as both thinkers spent time in the Alexandria library and were probably able to read hieroglyphs. Wasn't it also said that the great Homer spoke this unique language?

The first Christians and certain church fathers expressed some admiration towards hieroglyphs; but in 639 A.D., after the Arab invasion, night fell on the land of the Pharaohs. The establishment of a new Islamic state with radically different values from those of ancient Egypt resulted in changes in language, religion, customs, and even thinking patterns.

Did an oral tradition for reading hieroglyphs survive? It is possible, but unproven. In any case, Captain Bouchard, although brilliant, was incapable of reading the "Rosetta Stone." The scientists on the Egyptian expedition were no more capable. But France had finally discovered the missing link, and all hopes were allowed.

This joy was short-lived; as we know, Bonaparte's expedition finished with a military disaster, in which the general abandoned his men.

Our British friends took this opportunity to conquer Egypt, and the Rosetta Stone went to the British Museum in London, where it was exhibited with the inscription *"conquered by the British armies."* But all was not lost—copies had been made and a number of researchers used them to study the problem at hand.

There were many attempts at deciphering hieroglyphs during the early 19th century. In the middle of the 18th century, Kircher, a German Jesuit, had believed that hieroglyphs were symbols that could not be read phonetically, but he failed to decipher them. Although many scholars came to believe that the hieroglyphs would remain enigmas forever, the discovery of the Rosetta Stone led to a resurgence of interest. An Englishman named Young managed to decipher a few signs but soon found himself faced with insurmountable obstacles. It was Jean François Champollion who conquered this impossible task.

Born on December 23, 1790, in Figeac, Champollion wrote in one of his letters:

I belong to Egypt; it means everything to me. (November 24, 1828.)

A highly gifted man who was envied and hated by the scientific authorities of his time, Champollion lived to work. He was dedicated to accomplishing his extraordinary mission: finding the key to Egyptian hieroglyphs and returning them to the land of the living.

Champollion started studying dead languages as a child, and also learned Chinese and Persian. But, afflicted with ill health, he had to spend much of his life searching for money and an official post. He also lacked the original documents that some of his rivals, who didn't know how to use them, possessed. A number of times Champollion could not seem to uncover the hieroglyphs.

"I HAVE IT!," OR
THE REDISCOVERED HIEROGLYPHS

Paris, September 14, 1822 . . .

The Institut de France (French Institute) is at peace;

Champollion's brother is at work in his office, on this dull, grey, and passionless day.

Suddenly, the door opens.

An exulting Jean François Champollion runs in, yells, "I have it!" and faints.

His emotion was so intense that he remained in a state of lethargy for a few days. Lost in his own world, he was finally ready to decipher a few millennia of history and civilization. Luckily, the gods did not let Champollion leave this earth without sharing his vision, which was based on both an incredible amount of knowledge and extraordinary foresight.

To this day, the greatness of his discovery is staggering. Even with the use of computers, languages that are much simpler than hieroglyphs remain undeciphered. And it is only a human brain—or rather a human heart, so close was Champollion to his subject—that managed to lift the veil, thanks to a dazzling intuition that is still amazing.

Two theories had been common before Champollion. The first was that hieroglyphs were neither sounds nor letters like those of our alphabet, but symbols and images. For example, our duck may symbolize something, but what?

According to the second theory, each hieroglyph was a sound or letter. Our duck is an A or a B, or a C, but how can we tell which one?

Neither one of the two theories turned out to be completely accurate—they needed to be linked, and then deepened. That is what Champollion explained in his *Letter to the Baron of Dacier*, dated September 17, 1822, which in a sense marks the birth of the rediscovery of hieroglyphs:

It is a complex system, a writing that is figurative, symbolic, and phonetic all within the same text, a single sentence, I would even say a single word.

A brilliant statement, certainly, but, like Einstein's $E = mc^2$, it is not necessarily understood.

To clarify, let us now look at our duck in three different ways:

1. Just look at the head, beak, body, webbed feet, tail—it is undoubtedly a duck.

If we translate this sign by the word "duck," we are dealing with a *figurative* form of writing.

2. But it is clear in some sentences that the text is not talking about a duck; for example, when the fowl is drawn next to the sun, it is a symbol of the Pharaoh:

Here, the translation is not "duck of the sun" but "son of the sun."

In such a case, when the duck signifies something other than itself, it is used to mean the word "son." The hieroglyphic writing is then *symbolic*.

3. This duck sign is also a sound, which does not necessarily translate as "duck" or "son." In this case, we have a double sound, formed of S + A, which becomes SA, and can be used to write other words that have nothing to do with either "duck" or "son."

To attempt a comparison with the English, let's take two sounds, "con" and "front," which are two different words. But in a third word, "confront," you have the association of the two sounds, but not of their meanings.

Here, the Egyptian writing is *phonetic*.

It becomes easier to understand Champollion's brilliant equation after having studied the duck: Egyptian writing is indeed figurative, symbolic, and phonetic within the same word!

You can imagine Champollion's joy when, during his only trip to Egypt, he realized, by looking at the monuments, that he was right.

On January 1, 1829, at Ouada Halfa, across from the Nile's impassable second cataract, Champollion wrote this moving letter to the Baron of Dacier: *I am proud now because, having followed the Nile from its mouth to the second cataract, I am able to tell you that there is nothing to change in our* Letter

Medinet Habu. A monumental door covered in hieroglyphs communicates with the other world.

on the Hieroglyphic Alphabet. *Our alphabet is the right one, and is applied equally successfully to the old Egyptian monuments dating back to the Romans and Lagidae[1] and also, which is of greater interest, to the inscriptions found on all of the temples, palaces and tombs of the pharaonic period.*

Champollion also wrote a grammar, a dictionary, and a study on Egyptian divinities. He died, exhausted, on March 4, 1832, at the age of forty-two.

This authentic genius will never be sufficiently praised—without him, pharaonic Egypt might have disappeared completely. He brought an immense civilization and wisdom back to life; few men in history have done as much.

---

1. Greek kings who also ruled over Egypt.

2 | What hieroglyphs!

The word "hieroglyph" is not Egyptian, but a Greek term composed of the words *hieros* (sacred) and *gluphein* (engraved). In other words, the Greeks saw hieroglyphs as sacred engravings, which they are. But what did the Egyptians call their language?

They designated it by these two signs:

The first one, is a stick. It is used to write the words "stick" and "language."

The second, is a piece of cloth attached to a pole that is floating in the wind. This sign is used to write the word "god." When found on the facades of temples, these masts announced the divine presence.

So for an Egyptian, a hieroglyph is both "God's stick," on which one can lean to carry out one's life, and the "speech of God," which one must be able to hear.

To make the explanation simpler, we have somewhat reversed the expression. In Egyptian inscriptions, it appears in the following form:

Ramesseum. Thot, the master of hieroglyphs, writes names of the Pharaoh.

Why is the representation different?

⸠, "God," is placed ahead of ⸙, "stick," because that is how the scribe shows his respect for the divine, which must occupy the first place.

As for the three vertical strokes, they mark the plural and indicate that *all* sticks, *all* speech, and *all* hieroglyphs are being taken into account.

⸠ ⸙ ⫶

is thus read *God, the sticks* (or *the words*), which, in English, we would call: *God's words* = hieroglyphs.[1]

The attentive reader already knows the essentials, since he knows the name of the sacred Egyptian language as revealed by the ibis-headed god, Thot. His form of an ibis sign suggests the idea of "finding." And one can certainly agree by contemplating this extraordinary bird moving majestically through swampy terrain and finding his meal with a quick and decisive strike of the beak.

The old wise men described Thot as the "heart of light," the "creator's tongue," the wise scribe who could compose the annals of the gods.

Before writing anything, a scribe had to address a prayer to the gods; here is an excerpt from it:

O Thot, deliver me from useless speech. Be behind me in the morning. Come, you who are divine speech. You are a sweet fountain for the thirsty desert traveler. It is closed for the garrulous, and open for the silent. (Sallier Papyrus 1, 8, 2–6.)

---

1. For lovers of phonetics who are in a hurry, ⸙ corresponds to the three sounds: M + D + OO, which form the word MEDOO, and ⸠ also corresponds to three sounds, N + T + R = NETER. The whole reads MEDOO NETER, which reads: "God's words" or hieroglyphs.

DON'T TOUCH MY HIEROGLYPHS, THEY'RE ALIVE

We have all heard that Greek and Latin are dead languages, but this is not true of the hieroglyphs. Just look at a hieroglyphic text: it is full of animated characters, active men and women, birds, mammals, fish. And they continue to act, much as our duck continues to bite.

Pierre Lacau, a French Egyptologist, has written these pertinent lines:

For the Egyptians, every image is a living being, an active reality that enjoys both magical power and its own. And all of the signs in hieroglyphs are pictures. As letters, they have a sound value, but since they retain their precise and defined form, they also retain the power of their image.

For example, the lion has a sound value ROO, but it also keeps being a lion and in some ways retains the lion's power.

The Egyptians were so convinced of the power of the hieroglyphs that, in some texts, they cut lions and snakes in half to keep them from causing harm, or held reptiles to the ground with knives.

So, when in Egypt, do not get too close to a wall covered with hieroglyphs, and be sure not to touch. On one hand, you'll keep them from deterioration, and on the other you will avoid waking the sleeping snakes and lions.

The right way to approach hieroglyphs is with love and respect, for, to the Egyptians, only the written word ensured immortality. The "good son" was none other than the writing tablet, and there was no greater joy than to commit the writings of the sages to one's heart and mind.

In Hermopolis, in the Middle Kingdom, there lived a great priest of Thot named Petosiris, who was the master of hieroglyphs. If you visit his tomb, you will read the following words:

You, the living who are on earth, who will see this dwelling of eternity and will walk by it, come, and I will guide you in the way of life. If you listen to my words, if you understand and observe their meaning, you will find that this attitude will be beneficial to you.

Let us be attentive to this valuable counsel as we approach the hieroglyphs.

HIEROGLYPHIC WRITING, A VERY YOUNG OLD LADY

When did hieroglyphs first appear? It is hard to say. "King Narmer's tablet" and "The Scorpion King's club," which celebrate the victories of these very ancient pharaohs over the forces of darkness, are often referred to. Both kings lived around 3200 B.C. We believe that the hieroglyphic system was already in existence at that time. So it may have been born over 5000 years ago.

To quote Champollion: "Egyptian hieroglyphs always present themselves to us in a state of perfection, no matter how ancient the texts."

In fact, the writing of the old empire (circa 3200–2270 B.C.) during the time of the Great Pyramids is extraordinarily beautiful. Each hieroglyph is a small masterpiece, fashioned by the hands of a genius artisan. The notion of progress does not apply to hieroglyphic writing: it was perfect at the beginning, and never improved. In fact, when Egypt began its slide, the engravings were occasionally of lesser quality. On the walls of the great Greco-Roman temples such as Edfu, Dendera, and Philae, which were still active during the first centuries of our era, you can see some hieroglyphs that are heavy in design and not always legible, as if the sculptor's hand had lost its ability. But the hieroglyph's method of functioning had not changed.

This is an essential fact: until its last breath, the Egypt of the pharaohs kept its hieroglyphic "system," which was at the heart of its thought and civilization. Therefore, an initiate in hieroglyphs living during the 4th century B.C. could still read and understand writings composed a few millennia earlier, whereas we are barely able to read English writings of the 16th century.

While the spoken Egyptian language evolved greatly, as all spoken languages do, the principles guiding the use of hieroglyphs have remained unchanged since their origin. In some sense, this stability can be compared to the institution of the Pharaoh, Egypt's single political regime for over 3000 years that was imposed on invaders, be they Hyksos, Persian, Greek, or Roman.

By attacking the temples, which were the source of hieroglyphic culture, and by closing them, sometimes violently, Christians prevented the practice of this sacred language. Then the Arab conquest brought in another language that had no relation to hieroglyphs.

Nowadays, we are all in the same position regarding hieroglyphs. Whether European, Asian, African, Australian, or American, we must learn this language—since no one is born speaking in "hieroglyphs."

The situation was the same in ancient Egypt. The Egyptians spoke a vernacular that was not based on hieroglyphs, which were at the highest point of a culture that people needed to make efforts to reach. The spoken language of ancient Egypt is dead, forever gone, but the hieroglyphs have survived. And this language of the gods, this very dignified old lady, is now acting like a young girl in that she is being courted by more and more suitors who see in her infinite charms. Some, after having been bitten by the duck, have fallen into the arms of Sechat, the beautiful goddess of writing, who is seen tracing hieroglyphs on temple walls for eternity.

The last hieroglyphic inscription is dated August 24, 394

A.D., during the reign of Emperor Theodosius. It was not until 1822 and Champollion's extraordinary discovery that hieroglyphs were written once again. Today, many lovers of hieroglyphs are tracing these signs and attempting to translate them. Hieroglyphs are even being used in computer science, jauntily entering the third millennium.

Will this magical language have the power to regenerate itself?

As Isis resurrected Osiris, the hieroglyphic language preserves the secret of immortality. The great lady is attractive as ever.

3 How do they work?

YOU CAN FIND EVERYTHING IN HIEROGLYPHS

Hieroglyphs, we agree, are a sacred writing. But what is sacred enough to become a hieroglyph? According to the Egyptians, all the expressions of life are—from stone to star, including man and beast.

As Champollion noted, the hieroglyphs' ambition was to describe "all the classes of beings held by creation": the celestial bodies, the different aspects of nature, human activities, mammals, insects, fish, plants, minerals, types of construction, the most varied objects—reality in all of its diversity.

Hieroglyphs abolish time. These signs are beyond fashion; they are hard-wearing and anchored within their peaceful eternity. Their size matters little. Some hieroglyphs are minute, such as when a scribe writes them on a papyrus to trace one of the chapters of *The Book of the Dead*. Others are gigantic, such as the great pyramid of Cheops, which, itself, is a monumental stone hieroglyph.

As Champollion already understood, everything is a hieroglyph. In ancient Egypt, painting, sculpture, design, and architecture had a single goal: to embody hieroglyphs, which can be transcribed onto an entire temple, a statue, or a bas-relief as "sentences of monumental writing."

The mediums used were varied and numerous. Scribes wrote on stone, wood, leather, and, of course, the famed papyrus. While certain aspects of their technique are well known, no one has yet managed to duplicate the quality and original color. After all, some papyri, which appear so fragile, have survived over 3000 years!

During the ancient period, there were about 750 hieroglyphs. This basic "system" remained in force, without any change, until 551 B.C. with the closing of the last active temple, "Egypt's marvel," at Philae. That alone is a unique phenomenon, considering that other languages, such as Chinese, were originally composed of "hieroglyphs," but were quickly schematized to the point of being unrecognizable. Nothing of the sort happened to the Egyptian hieroglyphs. While a quicker writing form was being developed at the same time, the hieroglyphs remained immutable. No one would have dared modify these sacred forms, as they were life itself.

With time, the number of hieroglyphs grew. For example, during the New Kingdom, the horse hieroglyph was introduced, which was unknown at the time of the Great Pyramids.

During the time of the great Ptolemaic temples, at the end of Egypt's ascendance, there were thousands of signs. Why? Because the priests, who were still practicing the ancient and sacred language, knew that Egypt was about to die. Isolated and surrounded by the enemy's increasing hostility, they developed codes, a complex cryptography and writing that enabled them to conceal their thoughts.

The "sign games" multiplied, although the basic principles did not. This hieroglyphic burgeoning was an ultimate swan song, flamboyant and pathetic.

YOUR GOOD SIDE, PLEASE

Ah, that Egyptian profile! What has not been said, done, and written on the way people are represented in Egyptian art? From publicity to comics, the Egyptian in profile, flat as a sole, has continued to parade unshakably in the contemporary unconscious.

Are hieroglyphs really represented sideways? Well, yes. From the seated man 𓀀, to the standing mummy 𓀾, most of them are. According to the scribe, it is the easiest way to represent reality without deforming it. By presenting their best side, aren't hieroglyphs attractive?

Here's a question that could be asked on a TV game show: are any hieroglyphs shown in full face? The answer is yes.

Three examples:

𓁹

the face

𓅓

the owl

𓆣

the beetle (shown from the top)
Although the full face is rare, it is not forbidden.

HIEROGLYPHS CAN GO EITHER WAY

Which way do you write? What a strange question. Everyone writes from left to right, of course. Well, that's another idea we must abandon. Some languages, like Arabic, are written from right to left, which is supposedly less tiring.

And what about hieroglyphs? Even better! They are sometimes written from right to left, sometimes from left to right, sometimes horizontally, and sometimes vertically.

Let's look at things more closely and clarify the situation by taking our duck 𓅬, and adding a leg 𓂾.

To write "a duck and a leg," a scribe has a number of options:

1. →

Horizontally, and from left to right. There is a simple rule at work here: in order to read the inscription, you have to *go towards the signs*. Look them in the face because the hieroglyphs themselves are contemplating the beginning of the text.

2. ←

Still horizontally, but from right to left this time.

3. →

From left to right, and from top to bottom.

4. ←

From right to left, and from top to bottom.

A language in four dimensions, what could be better? The right and left hemispheres of our brain are thus working full throttle!

To simplify things, in this book, we will keep to our own habits and write the hieroglyphs from left to right. The ancient scribes would not condemn us, but they would find it too easy.

SPELLING—TO BE AVOIDED

There is at least one detail that should attract thousands of people to hieroglyphs: spelling does not exist. Thanks to hieroglyphs, there are no more difficult dictations. Liberty, in other words.

While you can't substitute one word for another, each term can appear in so many different forms that there is no need for a scribe to consult a dictionary for its spelling.

Let's take an example. To write "the living," based on

the hieroglyph ☥—the famous "looped cross" or "key to life" or "ankh"—the scribe can write:

☥ ❘

☥ ☥ ☥ 🐒

☥ 🐒 ❘

☥ ◉ ❘

☥ ◉ 🐒 ❘

☥ ◉ 🐒 🐒 🐒

☥ ◉ 🦅 ❘

☥ ◉ 🦅 🐒 ❘

with none of these being spelling mistakes. And that does not end the list.

Ah, the lost and blessed days of the hieroglyphs!

Another surprising detail is the lack of punctuation. No periods, no commas. In other words, there are no signs other than the hieroglyphs themselves. This is the decipherer's first problem: how do you separate the words from each other? Where does one word end and the next one start?

There is a way. You have to find what is known as the "determinant"—a hieroglyph that has a symbolic value and is placed at the end of a word to indicate the category it belongs to.

For example, ⚊, the rolled and sealed papyrus, means that the word it determines belongs to the category of abstract ideas. You can be sure that after ⚊, another word begins.

Reading hieroglyphs takes practice, of course, but with knowledge of the vocabulary, you can soon manage to identify the different words in a text, isolate them, and establish their relationships.

4 | A strange alphabet

We are now at the beginning of a great test: the discovery of the hieroglyphic alphabet, which has a certain number of surprises in store for us. We would have liked to avoid all this concentration and memorization, but the Egyptian gods are precise. It is something we must go through.

First of all, a simple truth: there are only consonants in this alphabet, no vowels. Why? Because the consonant does not get used up, whereas vowels are constantly getting modified by pronunciation in the spoken language. So while we become familiar with the timeless, solid, and intangible aspect of the hieroglyphic language, we will never know how vowels and pronunciation affected it.

For the moment, at least, everything seems simple. All you need to do is learn the hieroglyphs and figure out which letters of our alphabet they correspond to so that everything falls into place. Right?

Well, no. Some letters in the Egyptian alphabet have no corresponding letter to our own, and vice versa. So we will have to adapt.

Let us now examine each letter of the Egyptian alphabet in the order found in the dictionaries and lexicons used by Egyptologists.

A

This beautiful bird is a vulture, which, in medieval imagery, will become an eagle. To rise in the sky, Pharaoh sometimes takes the form of this bird.

Someone will be sure to say, but A is a vowel! No, that is a simple optical illusion. The A is not a vowel, but an aleph or, in other words, "a weak consonant." This is also true of the following letters, I, Y, OU. Despite these nuances, we will content ourselves with reading A (sounds like AH) as a beautiful vulture, and affirm loudly and clearly that this A is a consonant.

Valley of the Kings, Tomb of Rameses VI. The Pharaoh, shown in profile, makes an offering of fire.

$$i$$

Here is a flowering reed that we read as e (as in sit).

This hieroglyph incarnates the blossoming of life and nature made visible.

When there are two reeds,

$$Y$$

they are read as Y.

It is the same thing for two oblique strokes:

$$Y$$

The extended forearm, with the palm of the hand turned skyward, embodies action. It is read as Â.

$$Â$$

The small quail equals the OO sound (which is often written as W in phonetics).

$$OO$$

The spiral, which is one of life's purest expressions (think of spiral galaxies), is the other hieroglyph used to signify the sound OO. So the same sound can either have an animal form (the small quail) or a geometric shape (the spiral).

$$OO$$

$$\mathrm{J}$$

B

The straight leg and foot are read as B.

□

P

This hieroglyph represents a seat, a solid support, a base for a statue, and is sometimes compared to a stone. It is read as P.

F

The horned viper is a large hieroglyph; this animal's bite is fatal. It is read as F.

M

The owl, seen full face, is read as M. It is related to the interior, such as "in" or "that which is in."

M

Another way of writing the same sound; this hieroglyph represents an animal's rib.

N

This broken line does not only evoke water, but every form of energy. For example, when the goddesses hypnotized Osiris, they were holding this sign in their hands. This hieroglyph is read as N.

N

The same sound can also be written with the Pharaoh's red crown, which is adorned with its characteristic spiral.

R

This hieroglyph represents an open mouth. It is read as R.

H

This hieroglyph is the blueprint for a primitive building, probably a reed shack in the country. It is read as H.

H

This braided linen strand (where three numbers are inscribed: ONE lock, TWO "ends" on which it rests, THREE curls) is used to write a sound that doesn't exist in our language, but which we are also representing as H.

KH

We are still wondering what this hieroglyph really represents: either a placenta, or a sieve that sorts, separates, and keeps what is essential. The sound is similar to the CH in the German word NACH. For the sake of convenience, we are rendering it KH.

KH

Here is an animal's belly, with teats and tail. Again,

there is no exact approximation in our language, so we are calling it as a KH.

S

This hieroglyph representing a lock corresponds to the s sound.

S

The folded cloth, often held by dignitaries, is also used to write the sound s .

simplified as ▭

SH

Here, a basin full of water is pronounced SH.

Q

This hieroglyph represents a mound of earth; it is the sound Q.

K

This hieroglyph represents a braided basket with a handle; it stands for the K sound.

G

This jar support corresponds to the G sound.

T

This hieroglyph, in the shape of a superior semicircle that probably represents a loaf of bread, corresponds to the T sound.

CH

This sign is a yoke for an animal; it corresponds to the sound CH, as in chair.

D

The hand, with fingers together, the thumb on top, and the wrist, corresponds to the D sound.

DJ

The great cobra, raised on its tail, corresponds to the DJ sound, as in *jeans*.

(See tables on pages 35 and 36.)

ONE SOUND, TWO SOUNDS, THREE SOUNDS . . .

Thanks to our alphabet, we have discovered a very satisfying rule: one hieroglyph = one sound. But, as future scribes will notice, we have only looked at twenty-eight hieroglyphs!

THE EGYPTIAN ALPHABET AND
ITS PHONETIC EQUIVALENTS

Hieroglyph	Sound	Technical transcription used by Egyptologists (column reserved for future technicians)
	AH	ȝ
	I	ỉ
	Y	y
	Y	y
	Â	(
	OO	w
	OO	w
	B	b
	P	p
	F	f
	M	m
	M	m
	N	n
	N	n
	R	r
	H	h
	H	ḥ
	KH	ḫ
	KH	h̲
	S	s
	S	s
	SH	š
	Q	ḳ
	K	k
	G	g̱
	T	t
	CH	ṯ
	D	d
	DJ	ḏ

APPROXIMATE CORRESPONDENCES BETWEEN
THE EGYPTIAN AND ENGLISH ALPHABETS

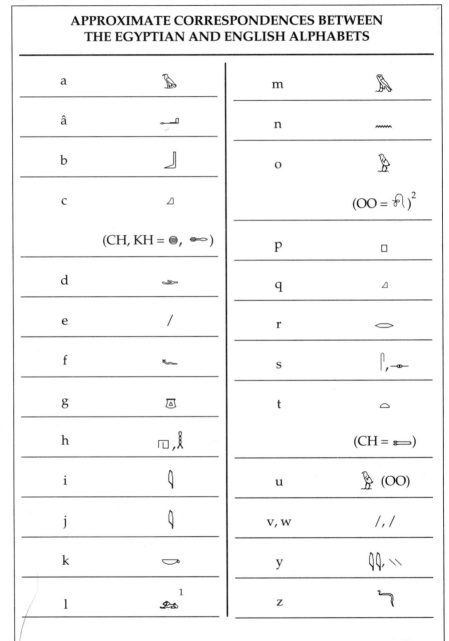

a	𓄿	m	𓅓
â	⌐	n	〰〰
b	𓃀	o	𓅆
c	◿		$(OO = 𓅱)^2$
(CH, KH = ⊜, ⇒)		p	☐
d	⇒	q	◿
e	/	r	⇔
f	⇝	s	⎮ , ⊸
g	⊠	t	◠
h	⬜ , 𓎼		(CH = ⇒)
i	𓇋	u	𓅱 (OO)
j	𓇋	v, w	/, /
k	⌒	y	𓇋𓇋 , \\
l	⇒ [1]	z	⟆

---

1. The lying lion is not a letter of the "classical" alphabet, but we know from the later texts that it was used to transcribe the sound L.
2. Same as above.

What about the others?

It's very simple, almost. The other hieroglyphs do not correspond to a single sound, but to TWO, THREE, FOUR, or more.

Let's take the eye, for example:

It is not a letter of the alphabet, and doesn't correspond to one sound, but to two, and is read as IR.

It can be broken down by using the letters of the alphabet:

IR   =   I   +   R

Or, the scribe can take the word apart within the sentence and indicate its alphabetic "components" so as to facilitate our reading:

I   +   R   =   IR (and not IRIR)

Let us take another hieroglyph that we have already seen—the "key of life" or "looped cross:"

It is pronounced ÂNKH, and breaks up into three sounds, Â + N + KH.

The scribe can sometimes break up the word by indicating its phonetic components, which alleviates any efforts of memorization if you know the alphabet.

Â   +   N   +   KH   =   ÂNKH

Unfortunately, in order to read a number of texts, we not only need to know the alphabet, but also how to read a lot of other signs that account for two or three sounds. That is why apprentice Egyptologists must learn long lists of signs and their phonetic correspondences with a lot of patience and perseverance.

5 | Our most common words are not hieroglyphs

TO BE AND TO HAVE:
HIEROGLYPHIC UNKNOWNS

If any two words are often used in English, they are "to be" and "to have" in their various forms. They are so present and necessary that it seems impossible for us not to use them. But there is no place for our two great stars among the hieroglyphs.

In the case of "to have," the situation is simple: the verb does not exist in hieroglyphs. The notion of "belonging to" can be formulated in a number of ways. If it is impossible to translate literally "she has a house," you can say: "her house, house for her,"and so on, with more nuances than in English.

As for "to be," the situation is not quite as hopeless. You cannot say, in hieroglyphs, "I am, you are, he is . . ." but you could say "I live" or "I exist," depending upon the degree of emphasis.

But, wait a second! There is another word that is formed by the two letters:

$$\text{I} \quad + \quad \text{OO} \quad = \quad \text{IOO}$$

It is not the verb "to be" in the strong sense, but a linking mechanism as in the sentence "The flower *is* in the field." Here, "is" is used for simplicity, when another word, such as "grows" or "blossoms," could be used as well.

39

Saqqara. The hieroglyphs in this inscription are written vertically and read from left to right.

YES AND NO, GOOD AND BAD

You would have to look long and hard to find words that would translate the "yes" and "no" we use so often. The Egyptians did not use these words. They preferred to say: "I have done this" or "I have not done that."

Y

can be translated into "absolutely, yes," but it is not a frequently used word.

N, NEN

This hieroglyph—both arms extended in a gesture of powerlessness—could be translated as a "no," but it is used more indirectly: to negate a developed sentence.

Neither yes or no, but rather an accomplished or unaccomplished act—that is the Egyptian position.

NEFER

well, good

The sign represents the tracheal artery, and the heart and lung system.

DJOO

bad

The sign represents a mound in the desert, an arid and desolate place, where dangerous and harmful forces abound.

Part Two

A LIFE IN HIEROGLYPHS

Karnak. Pharaoh, kneeling, makes an offering to Amon and receives life from the hand of the god.

6 | What is life?

LIFE IS A MIRROR AND A SANDAL STRAP

The best known hieroglyph appears to be the famous "key of life" or "looped cross" that we've already encountered:

$$\phi$$

ÂNKH

life

Why did the Egyptian sages symbolize life this way? What does this hieroglyph represent?

Ankh was a mirror made of copper, which was considered a celestial metal that had the ability to "trap" light. A ritual object, it was associated with Hathor, the goddess of stars and universal love.

It was also a sandal strap, seen from above.

An anecdote on this representation: When I was once talking with the famous physicist, Fritjof Capra, he asked me how the Egyptians defined life. I told him about the ankh's sandal strap and noticed his surprise.

He told me that there was a recent theory developed by physicists in the hopes of understanding this phenomenon known as "life." It was called *bootstrap*.

The Egyptians conceived of life, ÂNKH, as a power able to retain the original light. In the world of men, it was able to "give a path to men's feet," according to the lovely expression they used in texts—as long, of course, as your shoes are the right size and your laces are well tied.

♀, ÂNKH, is also used to write the following words:
—"the divine eye," as it is this eye that gives life
— "wheat," since it is an essential food
—"the crown of flowers," "the bouquet," since they are admirable expressions of life
— "the block of stone," as it represents the stability of life
—"the goat," since it is an animal that survives on practically nothing.

The sign ♀, ÂNKH, is also used in the idea of an oath, because giving your word means that you pledge your life; therefore, betraying your word means losing your life.

And finally, there is this surprising word:

It is composed of two ÂNKHS and two cow ears. We read it simply as "the living" and translate it as "the ears."

The old sages wanted to show that life enters through the ears. If they are open and perceptive, we live; if our ears are closed, we are incapable of living well.

In the words of the great sage Ptahhotep:

When the listening is good, life is good
He who listens is the master of what is beneficial
Listening is beneficial to the listener
Listening is better than anything else
That is how perfect love is born.[1]

For ancient Egypt, the first component of living was learn-

---

1. Christian Jacq. *L'Enseignement du Sage Ptahhotep.* La Maison de Vie, 1993, p. 151.

ing to listen, learning to hear, then learning to walk and move (the sandal strap), and finally becoming the mirror that captures the celestial light.

LIFE IS A FLOWER AND A HARE

"Life is not an existence" wrote a humorist, and Egypt does not disavow that statement. To "exist," or live life on this earth, Egypt uses two hieroglyphs, one animal and one plant.

⚘   , the flower

OON

to exist

🐇   , the hare

OON

to exist

The ancient Egyptians had a passion for flowers. Temple walls often display the offerings of flowers to the gods, while numerous paintings depict artful bouquets.

Wasn't it the dream of every Egyptian to have his own flower garden?

Ancient Egypt was in fact a real garden, constantly irrigated and cared for. By examining the bas-reliefs on tombs, you can experience the beauty and luxuriousness of the landscape. Cornflowers, mandrakes, lilies, and other marvels were not only beautiful, but also vital substances for the preparation of remedies.

Yes, existence is a flower in full bloom. But it is also a long-eared hare.

Here again, we find the notion of listening, to which the

idea of reproduction is added, since we know how prolific the hare can be.

The hare is a symbol of the god Osiris, who died and was reborn. By writing the hare hieroglyph, OON ("to exist"), the scribe subtly evokes the immortality of Osiris, who was assassinated and dismembered by his brother, Seth, but later reconstituted by his wife, the great magician Isis.

One of Osiris' most frequent names is:

OON	NEFER
the hare	*perfect*

It is an expression that is often translated into "the good being" or "he whose life was regenerated."

You can understand why each Egyptian wanted to become an Osiris; this way, his existence, if it had been good and just, could be eternal.

Valley of the Kings, Tomb of Thutmose III. Horus, the falcon, symbol of the king who was to unite Upper and Lower Egypt, is at the midpoint of a two-headed serpent wearing the crowns that symbolize both halves of the country. The snake wearing the red crown of Lower Egypt is related to the "key of life. "

7 Meeting Pharaoh

PHARAOH, "THE BIG HOUSE"

The word "Pharaoh" comes directly from the Egyptian

⊏⊐	𝍩
PER	ÂA
house	*big*

The hieroglyph ⊏⊐, PER, looks like the outline of a house. The hieroglyph 𝍩, ÂA, represents a column, which in this case means "big."

This expression indicates that the Pharaoh was not perceived as a simple political man, an individual holding power, but rather as a symbolic entity—a "big house" or "big temple," whose function was to welcome all of the divinities and people of Egypt, for whom he was a protective shelter.

Tanis. Two names for the Pharaoh: "he who belongs to the reed" and "he who belongs to the bee."

In the last hieroglyphic inscriptions, when no Pharaoh ruled over Egypt, the scribe could not indicate the name of the ruling king. The sculptors simply engraved ⊏⊐ ⌡ , PER ÂA, in the stone, keeping the generic symbol for all pharaohs.

PHARAOH IS A
BULRUSH AND A BEE

When visiting Egyptian monuments, one is struck by the frequency of these two hieroglyphs:

and

Both designate Pharaoh. Let us examine them one by one.

NY   SOOT
he who belongs to the reed

The expression is a complex one; it took many generations of Egyptologists to correctly decipher it. is the reed SOOT, which is made up of three sounds (, S + , OO + , T = SOOT, with the , T, written near the to facilitate our reading).

 is a tricky symbol, which is read N(Y) and signifies "he who belongs to" or "he who is in relation with."

Considering the order of the hieroglyphs, this word was long read as SOOTEN, but a more in-depth examination shows that the correct way to read was N(Y) SOOT: "he who belongs to the reed," with the word "reed" being placed at the head of the sentence to underline its importance.

Pharaoh is indeed "he of the reed," a plant that is particularly useful, since the reed as well as the bulrush and the papyrus—all of which are associated in this symbol—were used to make a large number of objects, from the scribes' writing support to the humblest pair of sandals.

From this angle, the Pharaoh is not only a thinking reed, but also an essential material, one that is in every way necessary and useful to his people.

BIT

he of the bee

This designation associates the Pharaoh with that extraordinary creature the bee, an animal that constructs its shelter according to rigorous laws of geometry, obeys an immutable hierarchy, and acts like an alchemist by producing the liquid gold that is honey. It also enables flowers to exist; if the bee disappeared, so would they. And let's remember that ⚶, the flower, means OON, "to exist." Thanks to Pharaoh-bee, life itself is possible.

Whether it is the famed royal jelly, with its exceptional energetic potential, or honey, the products of the hive and of the bee's work were considered rare and dear in Egypt. Despite the common perception, the Egyptians did not sweeten their foods with honey but with fruit juices (mostly from the date and carob).

Honey was only eaten in exceptional circumstances, and was often used as medicine. In fact, a recent study has demonstrated its surprising qualities as an antiseptic and healing substance. Pharaoh-bee is his people's healer, the one who takes care of their health.

The same root, BIT, is also used to write "the good action," "the fine character," "the person of quality." Isn't it, after all, how one would describe a good pharaoh?

"He of the reed" designates the Pharaoh as king of the South, or Upper Egypt, who wears the white crown ⚐.

"He of the bee" designates Pharaoh as king of the North, who wears the red crown ⚐.

Pharaoh's role is to unite South and North, and thus to wear both crowns, leading to the more common form 𝒴.

The two crowns are thus united as "the two powers," PA-SEKHEMTY, a term often transcribed as PSCHENT, which has shown up in some dictionaries, but has not managed to become an English word.

PHARAOH, L.H.S.

These days we love acronyms, and Egyptology does not pretend otherwise.

In many books, you can find the letters L.H.S. following the Pharaoh's name.

For the uninitiated, it is incomprehensible.

There is occasionally a note stating that the letters are the abbreviation for "life, health, strength," an old translation that is guilty of approximation.

What do the hieroglyphs say?

$$☥ \, 𝕻 \, ╒$$

As we know, ☥, ÂNKH, means "life";

𝕻, OODJA (a mechanism for preparing a fire), means "intact, safe, healthy and prosperous";

╒ is the abbreviation of ╒ ⸺⸺⤵, SENEB, which means "in good health."

These are the three good wishes that one offers to the Pharaoh so that he or she may always enjoy the three indispensable qualities for a happy reign: life, prosperity, and health.

One also wishes him or her the following:

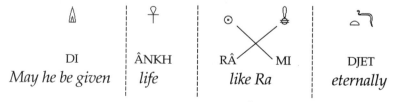

DI	ÂNKH	RÂ MI	DJET
May he be given	*life*	*like Ra*	*eternally*

The hieroglyphs actually say "Ra like" rather than "like Ra" in respect for the god of light, whose name must come before the preposition.

PHARAOH, MASTER AND SERVANT

Pharaoh is Egypt's master, its uncontested sovereign, because he has placed Maat, the rule of life and the universal balance, in his heart, therefore ensuring that tyranny could not result from his governance. One hieroglyph illustrates this idea quite well:

HEQA

to govern

is the shepherd's staff, the crook that is used to guide the flock and keep any of the beasts from getting lost. Long before Christ, Pharaoh was known as "the good pastor." The symbol was transmitted to medieval Europe to become the bishop's crosier.

But the term that most often designates Pharaoh is:

HEM

the servant

is a picket, which embodies verticality, straightness, the idea of an axis, of stability. Egyptologists have the bad habit of translating this hieroglyph HEM by the word "majesty," but its true sense is "servant." The word has also often (and mistakenly) been translated as "slave."

Pharaoh is HEM, the people's first servant, the only one whose duty is to serve permanently. Such was the grandiose meaning of the Egyptian monarchy: the one at the helm was to serve others, not himself.

HEM is frequently used in this expression:

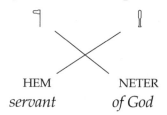

HEM	NETER
servant	*of God*

But NETER, "God," is placed before HEM, "servant," to show respect.

In most works, the expression "God's servant" is translated into "priest," which restricts its meaning. But the only HEM NETER in Egypt, the only "servant of God" who could officiate in temples, is the Pharaoh himself. During rituals, his image would descend from the sanctuary walls and incarnate as a priest for a short time.

PHARAOH THE BUILDER

A few days of travel in Egypt are sufficient to see that the pharaohs never stopped building domiciles for the gods. Although 90% of them have been destroyed, what has lasted leaves us speechless.

Pharaoh, as we have seen, is PER ÂA, the "big house" or the "big temple." So he himself is a building, and one of his main duties is to:

IR	MENOO
create	*monuments*

It is an expression that is often found on temple walls, especially in Karnak.

, the eye, is read IR, "to build, to do";

, the checkerboard, is read MEN;

○○○, the three vases, are used to indicate the plural, but

also form a pun with the word NOO, "the primordial energy," for the temples built by the kings served as a receptacle for this energy.

In the word MENOO, you find the root MEN (also found in the name of the god, AMON), which means "to be stable, well entrenched, durable"; and these are in fact the characteristics of the monuments built by the Pharaoh.

Let's identify three famous types of monuments:

𓉐

HOOT
the temple

It is a rectangular-shaped plan, with a door.

𓉴

MER
the pyramid

𓉶

TEKHEN
the obelisk

A CARTOUCHE THAT GIVES LIFE

In Egyptology, the cartouche gives life—it is an oval-shaped cord that is closed by a knot:

𓍷

Within this cartouche (read CHEN), the Pharaoh's name is written. An important detail: this cartouche can be extended to fit the length of the Pharaoh's name.

The sign symbolizes the part of the cosmos over which the Pharaoh reigns. This is the Egyptian response to the physicists who ask themselves if the universe is finished or expanding. In fact, the geometry of the cartouche is variable, depending on the number of hieroglyphs that compose the Pharaoh's name.

These cartouches have played a determining role in the deciphering process. They had, of course, caught Champollion's eye, as he knew the Greek transcription of the names of certain pharaohs. He was thus able to isolate certain letters, decipher them, and verify their use in other words.

A PHARAONIC WHO'S WHO

Here are the names of some of the stars of Egyptian history:

KHOOFOO = *Kheops*

KHOO	F	OO
protect	him	me

= "May he [the god] protect me"

KHAEFRÂ = *Khephren*

RÂ	KHÂ	F	= KHÂ FRÂ[1]
Ra	rises	he	

= "May he rise, Ra"

---

1. The god Ra is put at the beginning of the sentence for respect.

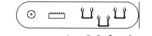

MENKAOORÂ = *Mykerinos*

RÂ	MEN	KAOO	= MEN KAOO RÂ
Ra	*is stable*	*strength*	

= "Ra's strength is stable"

HAT-CHEPESOOT = *Hatshepsut*

HAT   CHEPESOOT

= "First among nobles"

(or one who leads the venerable)

IMEN HOTEP = *Amenhotep*

IMEN   HOTEP

Amon   is in peace

(the hidden god)

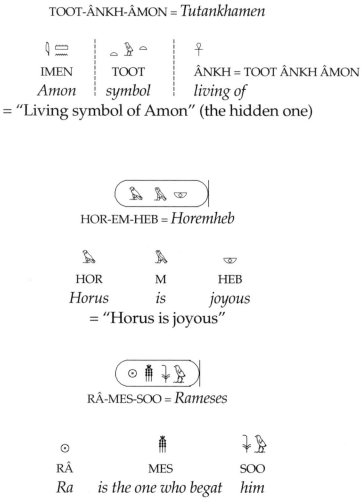

TOOT-ÂNKH-ÂMON = *Tutankhamen*

IMEN	TOOT	ÂNKH = TOOT ÂNKH ÂMON
Amon	*symbol*	*living of*

= "Living symbol of Amon" (the hidden one)

HOR-EM-HEB = *Horemheb*

HOR	M	HEB
Horus	*is*	*joyous*

= "Horus is joyous"

RÂ-MES-SOO = *Rameses*

RÂ	MES	SOO
Ra	*is the one who begat*	*him*

= "Ra is the one who begat him"

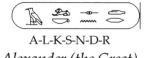

A-L-K-S-N-D-R
Alexander (the Great)

K-L-I-O-P-D-R-A-T
Cleopatra

As you can see, the names of the rulers of Egypt were not treated in the same way as those of the Pharaohs. The latter had specific meanings; on the other hand, a Pharaoh's name can and must be translated so that we learn the monarch's symbolic and profound being—his mission. When it came to the kings and queens, the scribes just spelled their names phonetically, using consonants alone.

8 In court with the dignitaries

The dignitaries surrounding Pharaoh constitute his court. The dignitary, or "great personage," is either a column, 𝄇, ÂA, or a swallow, 🐦, OOR.

Being important in the monarch's eyes thus requires either the rectitude and sturdiness of a column, or the grace and swiftness of a swallow.

The dignitary, the magistrate, the man with important responsibilities is called:

SER

This word, you can see, is represented by a standing person holding a long stick, which illustrates his authority. The word SER also means "to foresee, to see far ahead, to make known"; in ancient Egypt, governing meant having foresight.

A preeminent personage is represented by the front half of a lion:

HÂTY
the chief

A frequent title is:

Saqqara, Tomb of Mererouka. The noble is holding a command stick and is a hieroglyph himself, expressing the idea of grandeur.

HÂTY

the preeminent of arms

Â

whose actions are ahead

which designates administrators, mayors, and collective officials.

No matter how important, these officials must obey:

TEP

the head

(and)

RED

the legs

which is their duty to be accomplished, the right way of doing things, the appropriate custom.

Exercise 1

The following exercises are optional, of course. But who doesn't want to find out if he is becoming a good scribe? The answers are given after the twelve questions.

Question 1: Two young scribes are walking along the bank of the Nile. The first says to the second, "I've seen God." His friend looks at the facade of a temple and agrees. Why?

Question 2: ⌐, MEDOO, means "stick" and what else?

Question 3: How did the Egyptians write the word "life"?

Question 4: A stonecutter examines two stones from a quarry. On one is the sign ⌐, and on the other the sign ⌐. How does he know that one is good and one is bad?

Question 5: Why does a good student have ⌐⌐⌐?

Question 6: What do the following expressions mean?

⸙🦴 and ⸙🦴

Question 7: Who has the title ▭ ⌇ ?

Question 8: What three hieroglyphs are regularly placed after Pharaoh's name to ensure his life, wealth, and health?

Question 9: Why does the Pharaoh hold a scepter in his hand ⌇ ?

Question 10: Which hieroglyph represents the idea of "servant"?

Question 11: With which part of the body do hieroglyphs express the idea of creation, the verb "to do"?

Question 12: Why is it normal for a servant to obey a lion's head?

Answer 1: The scribe saw the hieroglyphic sign ⌐, a banner ornamenting the temple pylon.

Answer 2: "Speech."

Answer 3: ☥, ÂNKH.

Answer 4: ⌇ NEDER means "good."

⌣ , DJOO, means "bad."

Answer 5: Because the word ÂNKHOOY means "the ears," literally, "the living."

Answer 6: Both are read OON I and mean "I exist."

Answer 7: PER ÂA, "the big house" or "the great temple" is the Pharaoh.

Answer 8: ☥, ÂNKH, "life"

⚱, OODJA, "wealth"

𝄇, an abbreviation of SENEB, "health."

Answer 9: Because this hieroglyph, read HEQA, means "to govern."

Answer 10: 𝄇, the post, HEM.

Answer 11: By the eye, 👁 , IR.

Answer 12: Because 🦶, HÂTY, means "chief."

9

The hieroglyphic sky won't fall on our heads

THE SKY ON ITS FOUR PILLARS

Here is the sky:

This hieroglyph, read PET, represents a sort of table on four legs (of which we only see two).

When the god Chou, luminous air, separated the earth from the sky, he placed the sky on solid pillars so that it would not fall onto earth.

With that hieroglyph as a starting point, a number of celestial phenomena can be represented:

A five-pointed star hanging from the sky shows night.

Three broken lines emanating from the sky evokes rain. Although the sky, PET, is a masculine word in hieroglyphs, NOOT, goddess of the sky, is a feminine word:

⊃, the vase containing primordial energy, is read NOO; ◠ marks feminine words. ·

The starry sky has a wonderful name:

KHÂ   BA   S

a thousand is its soul

In other words, "the soul of the sky goddess is a thousand stars."

The expression is broken up as follows:

(lotus leaf) = KHÂ, "a thousand";

= BA, "soul";

= S, feminine third-person possessive pronoun, which refers to the goddess of the sky;

= the stars.

Valley of the Kings, Tomb of Rameses VI. Protected by columns of hieroglyphs, the sun boat crosses the subterranean universe as the resurrection of the sun is being prepared.

THE SUN HAS
A MEETING WITH THE MOON

RÂ

the sun

The word is composed of ⌒, R, the human mouth expressing the verb, and of ⌐, Â, the stretched-out human arm, which represents action.

Ra is the divine creative light, while the sun is represented by a famous word:

ITEN

which we know as ATON, the famous solar disk revered by Akhenaton and Nefertiti.

We can easily read the name of the moon:

IÂH

the moon

which is a masculine word, because in ancient Egypt the moon was seen as an aggressive, combative celestial power. There is nothing simpler than writing the "new moon,"

a sign many of us are familiar with from our calendars.

10 Taking the time of the hieroglyphs

THE YEAR, THE MONTH, THE DAY, AND THE HOUR

Egypt had established a certain number of divisions of time; here are the main ones:

RENPET

the year

This hieroglyph, which represents four sounds (R, N, P, T), designates a young shoot—symbol of the riches of nature.

RENPET means both "year" and "food," a good year being one in which the population is fed. It also means "the young, the rejuvenated," since each new year corresponds to a new birth, a new departure, after the extinction of the "old moons." The Egyptian New Year was celebrated throughout the country in July, after the Nile floods. Gifts were offered to the Pharaoh and people wished each other a good year:

RENPET	NEFERET
year	*good*

= "good year"

Saqqara, Tomb of Mererouka. This man, carrying plant offerings, suggests the happy seasons and the gentle flow of time.

ABED

the month

is written with a lunar crescent and a star. The Egyptian cal-
endar was based on lunar months and had a 360-day year.
Nevertheless, astronomers quickly understood that a 365-
day year was necessary to be in tune with cosmic rhythms.
The five supplementary days were considered a dangerous
period: the old year died, and the new one was not yet born.
Sekhmet, the terrifying lioness, chose that moment to send
her hordes of miasmas, diseases, and other miseries, which
Pharaoh repelled, thanks to the appropriate rituals.

HEROO

the day

is a word determined by the sun, and linked to the root HER,
"to be happy, satisfied."

GEREH

night

is a word determined by the nocturnal sky, from which hangs
a star, and is formed from the root GER, "the silence." In other
words, the day is the place of joy and night is the time for
silence.

OONOOT

the hour

This word is formed as follows:

OON	+	OO	+	T	=OONOOT

✳, the star, indicates the word "hour" and belongs to the category of cosmic phenomena; ☉, the sun, indicates that the word belongs to the category of temporal phenomena. The hour marks one's life (OON, "to exist") and reproduces prolifically, like the hare[1].

YESTERDAY, TODAY, AND TOMORROW

These three important words will help you to orient yourself within time. The first is easily read:

SEF

yesterday

☉ means that the word belongs to the category of temporal phenomena.

MIN

today

⚱ is a liquid-filled vase with a handle. It has three sounds, MIN.

DOOAOO

tomorrow

✳, the star, also has three sounds, D + OO + A = DOOA; ℮ = OO, DOOA + OO = DOOAOO, with the more precise meaning of "tomorrow morning."

---

1. The verb OON could also mean "to go fast," as an hour passes quickly.

EGYPT'S THREE SEASONS

We have spring, summer, fall, and winter—or four seasons lasting three months each. Pharaonic Egypt had three seasons, each lasting four months.

AKHET
the flooding
(from late July to late November)

The sign is a flooded area from which young shoots and blossoming plants grow.

It has three sounds: A + KH + T = AKHET

The scribe often writes the KH with the T to make it easier to read.

This season is of a feminine nature and named after the root AKH. AKHET could be translated as "the luminous one," "the useful," meanings that are particularly precise since it is about the blessed moment when the earth is irrigated by the floods, which deposit their fertile silt on the crops.

PERET
the "outing" season
(from late November to late March)

This season is considered winter and is when the wheat rises.

Its name is based on the verb ⌑, which has two sounds: PER (P + R). The scribe often adds ⌒ (R) to help in the reading. The ⌒ is the feminine T, and the ⊙ determines an aspect of time.

The verb PER, means "to rise, to come out." PERET is the

season when all that has been planted rises and comes out of the ground.

SHEMOO

the hot season

(from late March to late July)

This is harvest time, but it is also the season of intense heat. As the months advance, the previous flood recedes, and the people wait anxiously for the next one.

The word is composed of ▭, SH, 〰, MOO, and ☉, which determines a temporal aspect of time. What is strange is that this season is represented by a water-filled basin and a water sign when it is in fact the dry season. The sages were probably indicating that during this time the water held in basins should be used.

11 Nature in hieroglyphs

HOW BEAUTIFUL IS MY VALLEY!

A few common words will help us find our way in the Egyptian landscape:

TA

the earth

A flat piece of the earth, and three grains of sand represent it; this is the commonest way of designating the earth and the country.

TAOOY

the two earths, the double country

The expression designates Egypt in its totality, formed of two lands: Lower Egypt (the Nile Delta) and Upper Egypt (the Nile Valley).

KHASET

the mountainous country,
the desert region, the foreign country

Composed of three sand mounds, this hieroglyph represents the mountainous borders that encircle the valley, in both the west and the east.

AKHET

the light region, the horizon

This is the place where, every morning, the sun rises out of the darkness. It appears in the east between two mountains, having vanquished the demons of night. AKHET is also the name of Pharaoh's tomb, identified with a sun that rises eternally.

SEKHET

the field, the meadow

This hieroglyph represents the black, fertile, and swampy land from which three blossoming reeds and three reed, or lotus, buds emerge.

The sign ▨, CHA, expresses the notion of "beginning," by referring to the first manifestation of life, gushing forth from primordial waters.

▨, HA, "the papyrus plant," also means "behind, what is behind," in the sense of protection. Although they are no longer in existence, papyrus forests once served as shelters. It is in such a papyrus thicket that the goddess Isis hid her son, Horus, whom Seth wanted to kill.

THE EGYPTIAN LIVED
HAPPILY UNDER HIS TREE

The ancient Egyptians revered trees, which were much more common back then than in our time.

The sky goddess, Noot, lived in a sycamore. The Virgin

Saqqara, Tomb of Idout. There were many fish in the Nile, both in hieroglyphs and for food.

Mary remembered this while she was in Egypt and hid herself in a tree.

The name for tree is quite significant:

IMA

the tree

= I;

, the sickle = MA.

So we have I + MA = IMA. This root means "gentle, charming, pleasant, benevolent, well disposed." In other words, the tree is a symbol of the sweetness of life. Sitting below a tree, near the water, listening to the birds, contemplating the green of the fields and the twinkling of the Nile, is that not the ultimate delight?

The word MA is also found in the name of a tree that was essential to the Egyptians:

MAMA

Egyptian palm tree

It can be translated as "the very pleasant," "the delightful." Each part of the tree, from the fruit to the roots, is used. With the palm tree, one can make sandals, loincloths, and fans. The entire tree is used as a beam when building a house.

We also owe a Biblical expression to the Egyptians:

KHET   ÂNKH

the tree   *of life*

⟋⟍ , the tree branch, stands for two sounds, ⊜ , KH, + ◠ , T;
♀, the looped cross, has three sounds, Â + N + KH, as we have already seen.

This expression, "the tree of life," designates in particular the stem that supports plants, which give life and food. Pharaoh was seen as the tree of life in Egyptian society because he gave it spiritual and material nourishment.

THE FLOOD IS A
BOUNDING YOUNG MAN

Ancient Egypt was, as Herodotus once wrote, the gift of the Nile. Thus it is essential for us to know which hieroglyphs represented it.

The Nile's most common name is:

ITEROO

the river

I + T + R + OO = ITEROO

ITEROO is determined by ⟲, the sign of the canal, which shows that the word is part of the category of terms designating waterways.

The Nile, Egypt's only river, brought both water and prosperity to the country by flooding and depositing its fertile silt. This flood was an extraordinary phenomenon, which has now disappeared because of the Aswân dam.

The Egyptians gave it a masculine name:

HÂPY
the flood

H + Â + P + Y = HÂPY

HÂPY is determined by three wavy and superimposed lines, which symbolize water and waves.

On bas-reliefs, HÂPY is often represented as a potbellied person with heavy breasts and a head covered with aquatic plants, who carries rich foods.

However, HÂPY is based on a root that means "jumping, rushing." It is painted as an active young man jumping onto the shore to fertilize it. Unfortunately, HÂPY has disappeared. The "bounding one" is now a prisoner of the waters of Lake Nasser and must languish for his beloved Egypt.

12 The animals speak

Mammals, birds, reptiles, saurians, fish, and insects have inspired a number of hieroglyphs. The Egyptians were astute observers of nature and saw animals as the incarnation of a divine force, of a creative quality that had to be perceived.

STRANGE BIRDS!

The king of birds and protector of Pharaoh was Horus, the falcon,

whose name means "he who is far " (in the sky), "the distant one."

The vulture

is a synonym of the word MOOT, "the mother," for this great predator cares for its young with exceptional attention and diligence. It is also used to write the word "fear," as it is close to death.

Seen full face is the owl.

Besides being a letter of the alphabet, it is used to write "what is inner, what is on the inside."

The great ibis is an incarnation of the god Thot.

When it bends down to get its food, it is read GEM and means "to find," as the god of wisdom never misses his shot!

Another bird, a sort of stork, with a fleshy excrescence on its chest

is the soul-bird, BA.

The magnificent heron

is the Egyptian phoenix, the BENOO, which landed on the primordial mound that came out of the water on the first morning, and thus symbolizes abundance.

The next two birds are quite similar when written by scribes, but should not be confused. The first is the swallow,

which embodies the idea of grandeur: Pharaoh sometimes turns into a swallow to ascend into the sky.

The second one, which an apprentice scribe will draw with a forked tail to differentiate it from the swallow, is the sparrow (or the skylark), which means smallness, evil, sickness, and determines all words in those categories.

With the duck,

we discover how to write "son" or "daughter."

Quite similar in shape, the goose

Saqqara, Tomb of Idout (left). The head of a gazelle in light relief or perfection in hieroglyphs.

incarnates Geb, god of the Earth, while also being the representative of the fowl category. The goose can in addition represent the idea of being "well equipped," of "having what is needed," but it also embodies the concept of destruction.

When it has been trussed and plucked, the goose

is a synonym of fear.

A strange bird, the fledgling that is always moving, complaining, and asking for food

is none other than a symbol of the vizier, Egypt's prime minister! Is this an allusion to the fact that this dignitary, whose job was, according to the texts, "as bitter as venom," had to complain to his subordinates and beseech them to correctly carry out his orders?

BULL, LION, RAM—SOLID MAMMALS AT THE HIEROGLYPHIC POSTS

The king of mammals, and the mammal that represents the Pharaoh, is the wild bull,

a magnificent and powerful animal that a future monarch, such as the young Rameses II, learned to capture with a lasso in the desert. This bull is the KA, "the creative power." That is why Pharaoh wears a bull's tail attached to his loincloth.

This wild animal should not be confused with the ox, an animal that is eaten. The cow is a symbol of beauty, joy, and happiness. It is the cow's ear that was used to represent the idea of "listening, hearing, obeying" which had such great importance in ancient Egypt.

The ibex, carrying a seal around its neck,

represents nobility.

The lion, which is usually drawn lying down,

embodies vigilance, for, in Egyptian mythology, the lion's eyes are always open.

The front half of the lion represents someone preeminent—usually an important person, a chief—whereas the lion's lower half represents ideas of the extremity, the bottom.

The ram,

which embodies both Amon (the hidden god) and Khnoum ("he who makes"), is used to write the word BA, "manifestation." The ram's head, symbolizes the dignity that inspires fear.

The jackal, whether lying down or standing,

embodies the god Anubis, guardian of the secrets of the other world—the mummifier. The jackal is also a symbol of high dignitaries and judges. As for the domestic dog, it was loved to the point of being mummified and buried with its master. The cat, called MIOO, much like the sound it makes, was treated similarly.

The giraffe,

with its long neck, is a remarkable observer. It was used to write ideas like "to see far" and "to predict."

And what about the elephant? It had apparently disappeared from the Egyptian soil before the 1st Dynasty, but it was remembered, since it represented the first province of Upper Egypt, whose capital, Elephantine, is now Aswân.

To write about strength and power, the choices are numerous:

༐, a bull's head;
𓄀, a leopard's head;
𓄁, a jackal's head and neck;
𓄄, a bull's thigh.

How about writing about repetition?
One then writes 𓃾, the leg and hoof of a bovine, which is forever scratching the ground.

FROM CROCODILE TO BEE

The crocodile

𓆊

is a symbol of aggression and furor, but it can also embody the Pharaoh's bellicose and conquering aspects.

A more peaceful animal, the turtle,

𓆉

is sometimes considered evil or a symbol of resurrection, as is the frog.

𓆏

In ancient times, the Nile was highly populated with fish, and dried fish was the basis of the Egyptian diet.

The oxyrhynchus

𓆜

is designated the cadaver and all that is foul-smelling. According to the legend, this fish had swallowed Osiris' phallus after he had been dismembered, thus endangering his resurrection.

Other fish play a more positive role, such as the grey mullet,

which is used to write the word "administration" (of a province), and the *Barbus bynni,*

which provides help in the resurrection process.

The beetle,

is one of the most frequently used hieroglyphs, a real rabbit's foot which is used to write such concepts as "to be born," "to come into existence," and "to transform oneself."

The bee, as we have already seen, inhabits the higher realms, since it is a symbol of the king.

The modest grasshopper is also a hieroglyph. When the Pharaoh jumps from earth to sky, he turns into one.

13 Man and woman: An old story

AN INSEPARABLE COUPLE

In hieroglyphic writing, man and woman form a whole to symbolize "humanity":

The man, seen in profile, is seated. He wears a wig and a loincloth, and holds his right hand in front of him. The woman, also in profile, is seated, immobile, serene; she wears a wig and a dress. When the scribe is talking about humanity, of a human or social group, he uses the man and woman hieroglyphs, which cannot be dissociated from the entire human genre.

As Champollion wrote, the greatness of a civilization could be measured by the place it accorded to women; and in this area, Egypt could legitimately place itself in the first rank.

HUMANITY, OR THE TEARS OF GOD

The word "humanity" is written as follows:

REMECH

86

R   +   M   +   CH   = REMECH

The word "humanity" thus includes the human mouth, which symbolizes the ability to express oneself with words; the owl, a symbol of inner life; and the fetter used on animals, an allusion to the discipline necessary to living in society.

Furthermore, the word is formed from the root REM, which means "to cry." A text tells us that the sun fathered the human specie in a moment of sadness; humans were born from the creator's tears, who cried because of their behavior, their tendency to conspire, destroy, and hurt one another.

IS MAN A LOCK OR
THE FABRIC OF NOBILITY?

Man, the individual, is written:

It is composed of ⚬, the alphabet letter s, and the sitting man as determinant.

But what does ⚬ mean, if not a lock? We are faced with the locked man, closed in upon himself and his individuality.

To write "the woman, the female individual," you need to take the same letter of the alphabet and add a T, which marks the feminine, and then the sitting woman determinant:

SET

woman

There is another way of being a man or woman. Replace ⟶ with the other s, |, which represents the piece of fabric held by the nobility to symbolize its function.

This manner of writing "man" and "woman" is, however, much more rare than the previous one; does that mean that the individual is more often closed in upon himself than noble and sociable?

THE MALE DOES NOT HIDE

Man and woman, as everyone knows, are not completely similar. Ancient Egyptians were not prudish, nudity was not forbidden, and the hieroglyphs hid nothing. Thus the male was represented with all of his attributes.

This hieroglyph, which represents the penis, stands for "penis," "phallus," "the male."

A phallus ejecting a liquid means "to sire" or "to urinate." ⟶ can also be read as MET, which means "vessel" or "conduit" in any part of the body.

KHEROOY
the lower parts

KH	+	R	+	OO	+	Y	= KHEROOY

The word, meaning "the bottom parts," is being determined by the testicles, which were neither shameful nor

Saqqara, Tomb of Idout. A strange bird, this vulture is used to write the letter A.

noble, but simply low on the body.

It can also be translated as "the parts that carry," "the parts that support." The testicles are also called "the red ones" (INSOO) and "the purses, the bags" (ISOOI).

THE WOMAN IS A
FRESHWATER WELL

If the man is described by his obvious physical characteristics, the woman's sexuality is evoked much more poetically:

HEMET

woman

We are already familiar with ⌒, the feminine T, and the seated woman. But what does ♡ represent? It is a well full of freshwater and, by analogy, the female genitalia.

This ♡ has two sounds and is read HEM. This root also means "the rudder," "the artisan's skill." For after all, isn't the woman the rudder of her household? Doesn't she have the ability to direct the house?

In a hot country where water is the primary wealth, is it not moving to see the woman honored as the source of water?

Another word merits our attention:

HOONET

H   +   OO   +   N   +   T   = HOONET

HOONET means both "the young girl" and "pupil of the eye," an image that was kept in the Latin *pupilla* and our very own "pupil."

14 When the body becomes a hieroglyph

MEANINGFUL POSITIONS

Man can be seated 𓀀 and thus embody the word "man"; the seated woman 𓁐 embodies "woman."

When the man puts his hand in front of his mouth,

𓀁

it can mean a number of things.

First, it can mean anything having to do with eating and drinking, as well as anything having to do with speaking or holding one's tongue, and finally, with some terms related to thinking.

The seated man, with his hands open to the water coming from a vase, embodies ideas of "purification" and "purity."

𓀂

The collapsed, overwhelmed figure embodies ideas of "weakness," "fatigue," and the "rest" that is necessary in order to recover.

𓀗

Just because a man is seated does not necessarily mean he is resting, for the seated man carrying something on his head means "to carry," "to work":

𓀢

Aswân, Tomb of Sarenpout II. One can see a ram with its horns and an elephant in these wonderful hieroglyphs.

The naked child, with one finger on his mouth, embodies the words "child" and "being young":

The person seen sitting on his chair symbolizes the ideas of "nobility" and "being venerable":

When the man gets up, a number of different meanings appear.

The standing man, palms outstretched to the sky, means "to adore," "to venerate," "to pray," "to respect":

Standing, and with a single outstretched arm, means that he is calling:

When holding a stick, he embodies the idea of effort, and sometimes of violence:

If the man has committed too many grave mistakes, he finds himself upside down, which is the position of the damned.

For a civilization of builders, the act of construction was considered essential, and is represented by a man using a mortar and pestle, or by one who is building a wall:

A stick in one hand, a piece of fabric in the other, means that he is "great," "a noble":

Bent over and leaning on a stick, he becomes "the old one," "the ancient one":

The enemy, the troublemaker, and the rebel must be reduced to impotence. They are symbolized by a kneeling man with his hands tied behind his back:

The best fate is reserved for whoever has lived a life in

harmony with Maat, the goddess of truth. He will be mummified and then reborn. This hieroglyph carries the meaning "to die," but also "to sleep," before waking into eternity.

A VERY EXPRESSIVE FACE

The face, or parts thereof, also give us a number of hieroglyphs. ⊚ is "the head" (with a goatee); ◈, "the face" (seen full face); ⊂⊃, "the eye" (seen in profile).

The face, ◿, in profile, embodies "the nose," "breathing," and "joy"; ⊂⊃ is "the half-open mouth"; ⊐, "the upper lip and teeth"; ⌐, "the lock of hair"; ⌒, "the eyebrow."

STRENGTH IS IN THE NECK

We might compare a powerful person's neck to that of a bull's, and the Egyptians would not have disavowed this image, since they made the bull a symbol of royal power and virility. But when the scribes wanted to point to the neck as the seat of strength in hieroglyphs, they used another animal. To represent strength, they depicted the head and neck of a jackal:

OOSER

to be strong, powerful, rich

The animal embodies the god Anubis, the mummifier and guide of the souls of the dead. This hieroglyph may allude to the crucial moment in the mummifying process when the head is reattached to the body, thus reconstituting it for eternity.

Another way of expressing strength and power is:

$$\phi$$

SEKHEM

having mastery over,
exercising power over

This has to do with handling the scepter, often seen in the hands of Pharaoh or state dignitaries.

HAND GAMES

⟝ is the extended forearm, with the palm open towards the sky; the same arm, with its closed hand holding a stick, ⟝, embodies "effort," "strength," and "victory."

If holding a scepter, ⟝, the hieroglyph evokes the ideas of "to establish," "to direct," "to conduct." And in this form, ⟝, is the famous cubit (0.52 m). The extended arms, ⟝, express negation.

When raised, 凵, the arms form the sign KA; when down and making a digging gesture, ⟨⟩, they mean "to envelop," "to embrace."

The hand is represented as:

⟝, in profile and fingers tight. This fist, ⟝, means "to seize," "to grasp."

EXTEND YOUR HAND, TO OFFER

In these difficult times, we often see open hands asking for a handout. That gesture was unknown in ancient Egypt— extending a hand usually meant one was giving someone a loaf of bread.

DI

to give, to offer

To give is to offer, to allow the other to eat and be well, for there is no selfish joy, according to the ancient sages.

The generous man is AOO DJERET, "he who has the long hand." For the Egyptians, the longer the hand, the greater the offering.

A short text, often found on tomb walls, shows how much the Egyptians concerned themselves with generosity:

N	SEDJER	S	HEQEROO	M	NIOOT	I
not	*night will pass a man*		*hungry*	*in*	*city*	*mine*

= no man will spend a hungry night in my city.

USING OUR THUMBS

To work well, one must be balanced, have a sense of fairness, and not betray justice. A single term expresses all of these notions:

ÂQA

to be precise, exact, meticulous

"Using your thumbs," then, for an Egyptian, means to work diligently.

Two thumbs appear in another word:

METER

to witness

Continuing with popular expressions, the Egyptian term "to witness" means that, to have the courage to do so, you must not hesitate to show your thumbs, and to be exact and precise in your declarations.

USING OUR LEGS

The sign ⌂ is quite frequent: the moving legs mean "coming, going," and determine all of the words that fall under the movement category.

⌂ ⌐ means "coming and going," "coming in and out." The straight leg, ⌋, is both "the leg," "the foot," and "the place" (where the foot rests).

When the leg bends, ∬, it still means "leg" or "foot," but also "knee" and "to move quickly."

When the leg is topped with a vase from which water flows, ⌠, it is the symbol of purification.

And finally, the toes, 𝌡 , embody the idea of attaining one's goal.

Exercise 2

Question 1: Why does ⚏ have stars?

Question 2: Does one see ⊒ during the day or night?

Question 3: What did Egyptians say to wish each other a happy new year?

Question 4: Why did the mother worry about the end of the ⌢⋆ ?

Question 5: Is it good to sleep during the ⊡⌇⊙ ?

Question 6: Why hope that ⚲⊙ MIN will be better than ∥⊙ SEF, and not as good as ⋆⊙ DOOAOO?

Question 7: Should one cover up during the ⌷〰⊙ season, SHEMOO?

Question 8: Is it better to live in ⚌, TA, or ∿, KHASET?

Question 9: Where does one find the greatest sweetness?

Question 10: Why did the Egyptians wait for 𓀀𓉐𓈖 impatiently?

Question 11: Which hieroglyph symbolizes the mother?

Question 12: Which animal symbolizes nobility?

Question 13: Which animal symbolizes the capacity to predict?

Question 14: How does one write "to be born," "to transform"?

Question 15: Which hieroglyphs are used to write "man" and "woman"?

Question 16: What does ⛉ mean?

Question 17: What does ⅂ mean?

Question 18: How does one write "to give, to offer"?

Answer 1: Because Noot is the goddess of the sky.

Answer 2: The day, since ⌒⊙, RÂ, is the sun (written in its abbreviated form in the question, without its determinant).

Answer 3: 𓇥 ⌒ RENPET NEFERET, "Year good!"

Answer 4: Because this hieroglyph is read ABED and means "the month."

Answer 5: Except for nap time, no, since it stands for HEROO, day.

Answer 6: Because MIN means "today"; SEF, "yesterday"; and DOOAOO, "tomorrow."

Answer 7: All you need is your sunscreen, since SHEMOO is the hot season—Egypt's long summer.

Answer 8: TA, "the land, the country," is propitious to the living, and KHASET, "the desert," to the dead.

Answer 9: Under 𓇋𓐠𓏲, IMA, "the tree," whose name is formed from the root IMA, "sweetness."

Answer 10: Because HÂPY are the Nile floods.

Answer 11: The vulture, 𓅐, MOOT.

Answer 12: The ibex, 𓃵.

Answer 13: The giraffe, 𓁴.

Answer 14: With the beetle, 𓆣, KHEPHER.

Answer 15: ⚊ S, or ⎪ S.

Answer 16: The woman (with the determinant 𓁐)—the word is read HEMET.

Answer 17: The sign is read OOSER and means "to be strong, powerful, rich."

Answer 18: With this sign, ⚊◻, DI.

15 Love in hieroglyphs

LOVE? A HOE, A CANAL, AND A PYRAMID

MER

to love

, the hoe, used to till the soil, has two sounds: MER. The word "love" is determined by the man holding his hand to his mouth.

Why write such an important verb this way? Because the hoe, which the Pharaoh was the first to handle when digging the trench of the first temple, is used to inaugurate a site, and is therefore something durable. When handled by the peasant, the hoe opens the earth and makes it fertile.

The ancient Egyptians did not consider the sentimental aspect of love to be the most important; they were more interested in its long-lasting and profound aspects.

A synonym, MER, means "the canal"; after all, isn't love a circulation of energy—the canal by which a vivifying force, as important in its own way as water, passes?

Another synonym: MER, "the pyramid," is a symbol of the love that links Pharaoh to the gods.

Hoe, canal, pyramid. . . . It is the constructive aspects of life that these hieroglyphs put forth. But, the same root,

Valley of the Kings, Tomb of Thutmose III. Isis, the ideal woman. Kneeling on the hieroglyph that symbolizes gold, she is preparing Osiris' resurrection.

MER, when determined by an evil bird, takes on the meaning of "sickness." One can, no doubt, die from love.

LOVE, MY SWEET LOVE

Carnal love, accompanied by pleasure and sweetness, is symbolized by this hieroglyph:

NEDJEM

soft, pleasant

This sign represents the fruit of the carob tree, a beautiful tree that was once common in the Egyptian landscape. It was delicious and gave a sweet juice.

The pleasure of loving was called NEDJEM-NEDJEM, "sweet-sweet."

The hieroglyph for "making love" is:

NEHEP

The root NEHEP also means "to take care of," "to have pulsations," and "to moan."

Let the man be careful, though, not to look only to his performance, because there is little distance between ÂBÂ, "the phallus," and ÂB, "boastfulness."

Egyptian lovers used pet names with each other, such as "my little bird." This little bird, however,

SHERI

is the bird of evil and means "to be small," "to be weak."

The term "knowledge" is not always about high speculation, but can also designate a person whom you know intimately—the difference is made quite clear by the hieroglyphs.

REKH

to know (a subject, an area)

is determined by the sealed papyrus roll, a symbol of abstract ideas. The same word,

REKH

to know (a loved one)

is determined by a very concrete symbol of knowledge.

TO BE HAPPY, LET US SEE LIFE IN GREEN

OOADJ

papyrus, to be vigorous

This hieroglyph is a papyrus stem. OOADJ means "papyrus," but also "to be green" and "to be vigorous, healthy, wealthy, happy."

Happiness is being as green as a papyrus. The sage Ptahhotep recalls that a good word is more hidden than the "green stone," a symbol of happiness. The cobra goddess OOADJET protects Pharaoh and gives Egypt its greenness. By its dominant color, nature is the most perfect expression of expansion.

AOOT   IB

largeness of the heart

This means "joy, happiness," for a tight and narrow

heart is very sad. To laugh is written as follows:

SEBET

The word is determined by a tooth, which is uncovered when one smiles.

A common expression, dear to the hearts of many Egyptians:

IR	HEROO	NEFER
make	*one day*	*happy*

means that a day was good, beautiful, and perfectly constituted (NEFER), with every act perfectly in place.

Could happiness be complete without friendship?

ÂQ	IB
the one who penetrates the interior	*of the heart*

is a real friend, the one you can count on.

16 Parents and children

MY FATHER, THIS SNAKE

IT

the father

This hieroglyph is one of the better traps for a beginning Egyptologist. Since we now know something of the alphabet, we can take this word apart as follows:

⸲	=	I
⌒	=	T
⸴	=	F
I+T+F	=	ITEF

But that word doesn't exist! What happened? Is our alphabet wrong?

Let's go back to the hieroglyphs. In fact, in this word, and in this word alone (perhaps because of the difficulty of being a father), our ⸴, the horned viper, is not read as F, and is not a letter of the alphabet, but a symbol that represents "the father."

The word is read IT, and is determined by the horned viper. The father is thus a snake.

Did the Egyptians see the father as a venomous reptile,

particularly dangerous, and able to give death to his child?

Neither the texts nor the bas-reliefs evoke such a horrendous situation. They allude to a mythological serpent, "the creator of the earth," considered a protector of humanity—a symbol of positive energy circulating in the ground to fertilize it. A synonym, IT, means "barley," the fundamental food that the father must give his child.

MY MOTHER, THE VULTURE

MOOT

the mother

No difficulty here; the alphabet poses no traps.

M   +   OO   +   T   = MOOT

The word is determined by the female vulture, which can be read as MOOT on its own.

If the father is terrestrial (the snake), the mother is celestial, but it is a vulture, an animal that we don't find particularly appealing. Nevertheless, for the Egyptians, it embodied the most excellent mother, for the bird gave its young ones exceptional care. MOOT is the name of the great goddess of Karnak, Amon's wife.

The teachings of hieroglyphs are remarkable: although she is celestial, the mother vulture does not hesitate to land to dismember carrion and transform death into a vital food, so as to transmit life.

Isn't it amazing how, in a few hieroglyphic terms, the mysteries of the human condition are evoked?

I SWALLOWED THE BROAD BEAN

The word 𓇋𓏲 𓂋𓂻 is quite rich in meaning.

I	+	OO	+	R	= IOOR

The term is determined by the woman, who is still seated in profile and wearing a wig, but now has a rounded stomach. No doubt about it, the snake father slithered into the vulture mother and she is now IOOR, "pregnant."

And another word IOOR means "broad bean."

There are a number of different ways of announcing the blessed event in English. In the era of the Pharaoh, a woman telling her husband she was pregnant would probably have said something along the lines of "Darling, I swallowed the bean."

HORNS . . . TO OPEN EVERYTHING

Horns had an excellent reputation in ancient Egypt. Great divinities like Amon, Osiris, or Khnoum, all wore horns. And the pair of horns was also used to write important words.

OOP

OOP means "to open," "to inaugurate," in various expressions.

OOP means to open the woman's womb during labor.

OOP is also opening the face, mouth, and ears during the resurrection rites practiced on a mummy.

OOP means to start the new year, inaugurate the ceremony.

OOP means opening the road.

This idea of "opening" also implies that of "discerning, judging, separating, distinguishing," because the two horns denote the two aspects that the intelligence can discern without dissociating.

TO BE BORN AND GROW,
THREE SKINS AND A BEETLE

Once the womb is open, birth can happen:

MES

to be born

The second hieroglyph represents a squatting woman, her arms dangling in fatigue; her newborn's head and hands hang below her. Egyptian women gave birth standing or squatting, assisted by a number of midwives.

The first hieroglyph, represents three animal skins linked at the top, and is pronounced MES.

Why is this strange symbol, which means "born of," applicable to both the Pharaoh, born of the gods, and to a child born of parents? Birth is conceived of as coming out of three skins, three envelopes, which probably correspond to the triple conception of the universe: the sky, the intermediary world, and the earth. A text reveals that "all gods are three," since the number embodies a well-constructed totality.

There is another way of describing birth—with a beetle or scarab:

KHEPER

to be born, to come into existence,
to become, to develop, to transform oneself

To be born is not enough: one must grow and develop. The Egyptians saw the beetle as a sort of alchemist; by rolling a ball of manure between its legs, it prepared for the arrival of a new sun. That's why the morning sun is compared to a beetle, the symbol of a life coming out of the darkness; the beetle god is called Kheper (often written Khepri).

When an Egyptian wanted to allude to his career and life, he would say, "I've accomplished the beetles," which means happy mutations and transformations.

THE BREATH OF LIFE,
OR THE WIND IN THE SAILS

If water is indispensable to life, another element frequently mentioned by the Egyptians is the breath of life.

To translate this concept, without which no existence is possible, the following hieroglyph is used:

TCHAOO

air

It is a mast and sail swollen by the wind, which cannot be seen, but whose action is obvious and thus very real. This hieroglyph is used in the expression "the breath of life," which the divinities offer to the Pharaoh so that he may in turn offer it to the people.

One of the reborn's greatest joys is to enjoy this breath for eternity. It is also the essential element for the newborn. Once he has been given the breath of life, he can face the first struggles of existence.

A SON OR DAUGHTER,
AND THE RETURN OF THE DUCK

The child is born, has enjoyed the breath of life, and is starting to grow. But is it a boy or a girl? Our duck returns. is read SA.

If it is a boy, we have:

SA

the son

The duck is followed by a boy.
If it is a girl,

SAT

the daughter

the duck is followed by the feminine T and a seated girl.

THE IGNORANT CHILD

The most common way of designating a child is:

KHERED

the child

KH + R + D = KHERED

The word is determined by a naked child with a dangling arm, and his right hand on his mouth to show that he is silent.

Another way of designating a child is:

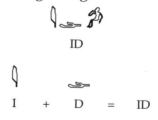

ID

I + D = ID

The word is determined by the same child. But ID also

means "the deaf one." In Egypt, the child was not considered an idol for whom all had to be sacrificed, but a being in need of education because it is naturally deaf to wisdom. According to Ptahhotep, one should "open the ear on its back."

Ignorance is written:

KHEM

to ignore

KH   +   M   = KHEM

The word is determined by the outstretched arms, which is a sign of negation and impotence. KHEM, "to ignore," is also "to destroy, hurt, exclude, be dry, arid." That, according to the Egyptians, is where ignorance leads.

That is why education holds such an essential place in Egyptian society, and there is no greater science than that of hieroglyphs, since it allows for the knowledge of reality in its most hidden aspects.

17 | **Name of names**

The name is composed of two hieroglyphs that are easy to decipher:

REN

the name

To give a name is a fundamental act in Egyptian life because REN, "the name," is an aspect of the person that will survive after his physical death, if the tribunal of the other world recognizes him as a righteous being.

Notice that REN is composed of ⌒, the human mouth that expresses the verb, and of ⌇, the energy. To name is to formulate an energy; the Egyptians believed that knowing the name of something or someone came close to knowing its, his, or her true nature.

There was a great quantity of names[1]:

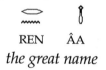

REN   ÂA

the great name

---

1. In hieroglyphs, the adjective is placed after the noun, so one would say "the name great, the name little."

Karnak. A monumental image of the couple. The wife is standing on Pharaoh's feet and enjoys his protection.

REN   NEDJES
the little name

REN   NEFER
the beautiful name

is the lasting name of a person who has been resuscitated.

REN   MAA
the real name

is the name recognized as just and true to Maat's rule—not a "real" as opposed to a "fake" name, which would have been an unthinkable notion in ancient Egypt.

REN   SHETA
the secret name

is given to the child by his mother or a priest. It was only revealed to the child upon attaining adulthood, if he was judged worthy.

There was no worse punishment, during a trial, than to take away the criminal's name and replace it with one that he would have to carry for eternity. For example, the conspirator who had tried to assassinate Rameses III was given the name "He who hates light" by his judges.

"To pronounce" is said:

DEM   REN

The word DEM, symbolized by the knife, means "to cut, to sharpen." One must "sharpen the name" and "carve" it so as to make it precise and effective.

A word that is close to REN

RENEN

means "to raise, to nourish at the breast." Giving a name is a way of nourishing a child, raising him, and allowing him to develop. The goddess of the harvest, a female cobra whose protection was very much sought after, is called RENENET, "the nourisher." From an Egyptian point of view, "naming" and "nourishing" are inseparable.

THE LAST EGYPTIAN NAMES: SUSAN AND ISIDORE

A few Egyptian names have traveled through the centuries to arrive in our European languages in a more or less recognizable form. This is true of these two first names.

SESHEN

she of the lotus = SUSAN

S + SH + N = SESHEN. The word is followed by a lotus

West Thebes, Tomb of Rameses III. At the bottom of the column are hieroglyphs of the New Kingdom. One recognizes the outstreched hand and the legs.

flower, which women wore as an ornament.

Isidore is not as popular a name as Susan. Its derivation is less obvious, but just as certain. It comes from Isis-dore, "the one that Isis gave."[1] The lucky few named Isidore are thus the descendants (by name, at least) of the last initiates of her secret rites.

The names Humphrey and its Italian version, Onofrio, are both adaptations of the Egyptian OON-NEFER, "the good one, the perfect one," an epithet frequently found near the name of the god Osiris.

---

1. In hieroglyphs, we have PA-DI-ASET, "the given by Isis," "the one given by Isis." PA, "the," has disappeared. ASET has undergone a phonetic transformation to become Isis, Isi. The Egyptian Di has become "dore"; hence, Isi(s)-dore, the goddess's name being placed first.

18 | In hieroglyph school

TEACHING IS A LUCKY STAR

"To teach" is written:

$$\mathbb{N} \mathbb{J} \mathbb{A} \mathbb{H}$$

SEBA

to teach

$$\mathbb{N} \qquad \mathbb{J} \qquad \mathbb{A}$$

S + B + A = SEBA

The word is determined by a man handling a stick, which stresses the need for effort.

When written with a star as a determinant, the same word takes on another meaning:

$$\mathbb{N} \mathbb{J} \mathbb{A} *$$

SEBA

star

But the word "to teach" can also be written:

$$\mathbb{N} \mathbb{J} \mathbb{A} * \mathbb{H}$$

This hieroglyph links both ideas: teaching certainly

takes effort, but it also gives light, a star, to the student in order to guide him.

SEBA is also "the door," and we can easily understand that teaching opens the door to knowledge.

Saqqara, Tomb of Ti. A seated man, with a viper on his head, expresses the idea "to carry."

THE VIRTUES OF A GOOD STUDENT:
SILENCE AND LISTENING

The Egyptians saw the long-winded as wicked, and compared them to a dry tree. To learn, one must first be silent:

GER

silence, to be silent

G + R = GER. The man's hand is on his mouth to show that he is silent.

But silence is not sufficient; he must also learn to listen:

SEDJEM

ear

This ear is that of a cow rather than a human, and has three sounds (S + DJ + M = SEDJEM). It is the great ear of the sacred animal of the goddess Hathor, queen of the sky. The ears are called "the live ones."

INFORMATION:
AN AFFAIR OF THE HEART

SOODJA   IB

to make happy   *the heart = to inform*

$|$ = S; $\mathcal{R}$ = OO; $\underline{\mathcal{U}}$ is a stick pushed into a piece of wood to make fire. The sign has two sounds, DJ + A = DJA; ⟶, the sealed and rolled papyrus, indicates that the word is an abstract idea;

�, the vase that symbolizes the heart, is read as IB.

The entire expression is thus read SOODJA IB, "making the heart happy" through instructing and informing.

From the Egyptian point of view, all accurate information makes us happy. But we must have the essential organ, this IB, which is not just the heart as a physical organ, but rather the conscience seen as a receptacle of thought and knowledge. In Egypt, there is no knowledge without heart.

CHARACTER NEEDS WORK

There is nothing better for shaping the character than this, ⳼ , a carpenter's scissors. It is read MENEKH.

Followed by the abstract sign ⚊ and the word ⳼ ⚊, MENEKH means "powerful, effective, well made, dignified, worthy of confidence, excellent, well adjusted."

By using the scissors, it is possible to cut a piece of wood and obtain:

ⵁ

QED

the character, the state of mind

which is a stake that you can plant solidly in the ground.

According to Egyptian sages, character must be worked on like a material and, to be of good quality, must be a solid support to its proprietor.

SEEING CLEARLY—A DRILL!

Listening is one decisive step on the path to knowledge; seeing is another.

MA

🌙, the sickle, has two sounds: M + A = MA; 👁, the eye, indicates that the word is somehow related to vision.

Why the sickle? It shows that vision is an act of separation (we have two eyes), which provides an essential nourishment.

The following hieroglyph represents seeing very clearly and having a piercing eyesight:

OOBA

The sign represents a drill as well as the hole it has made; thus, we are seeing it in action.

OOBA IB, "to pierce the heart," means "obtaining someone else's secrets."

OOBA HER, "piercing of eye," means "he who sees well," "the lucid one."

19 Reading and writing

READING IS LIKE
HAVING A WELL-FILLED WATERSKIN

CHED

reading

The hieroglyph is a filled waterskin and has two sounds, CH + D = CHED. It is followed by a picture of a man holding his hand to his mouth to show that reading requires silence as well as being a form of nourishment, like the fresh and beneficial liquid found in the waterskin. What is more refreshing than an interesting text?

So the good reader has a well-filled waterskin. Whoever can read will not die of thirst. There is only one remedy for a dry heart, and that is reading.

The root, CHED, also means "to breast-feed" (here again is the notion of a beneficial liquid), "to educate," and "to dig." By reading, we deepen our understanding of texts and ideas. In other words, we dig deeper.

WRITING IS DRAWING

In order to appreciate hieroglyphs, we must draw them. The old scribes would not have liked our typewriters and computers, because they keep us from really working with our hands. To write is to know how to draw and how to trace forms on a support (wood, stone, paper, etc.). It makes our hands intelligent and wise. The hieroglyph "to write" is quite meaningful:

SECH

writing, drawing

This hieroglyph, which has two sounds (s + ch = sech), represents the writing materials that the scribe needs and carries with him wherever he goes. They include:

—the carrying case holding pointed pieces of reed, much like the later European goose feathers;

—a jar of water to thin out the cakes of ink;

—a wooden palette, with two holes for the cakes of ink, one red and one black.

A small cord ties all of these things together when the scribe is traveling. The palette serves as a support. The scribe dilutes the cakes of ink with a small brushed dipped in water. He dips the reed in the ink and writes.

MAIL

The Egyptians often exchanged letters, not only between the living, but also between the living and the dead.

A widower could write to his deceased wife so that she would stop persecuting him since he'd been a model husband.

A letter started with the following expression:

SOODJA   IB

rejoice   *the heart*   = "to inform"

In other words, "Let me bring gladness to your heart (by

letting you know that . . .)." The letter usually ended with:

NEFER   SEDJEM

may be good   *the understanding*

In other words, may the contents of the letter be properly understood.

Valley of the Kings, Tomb of Rameses VI. This scene depicts the rebirth of the sun in the shape of a winged beetle, the symbol of metamorphosis.

20 Counting and measuring

COUNTING TIME

For counting there is a very simple word:

IP

*counting, fixing, distributing, examining,
taking inventory, measuring*

The term is composed of:

I + P = IP

plus the sign of the abstract, ⚊ . It is used in an expression that you can see on the walls of the great temple of Karnak:

IPET	SOOT
she who inventories	*the places*

This means the temple (a feminine word in Egyptian) that inventories all the other Egyptian temples and ranks them accordingly.

We can easily identify the components of the word IPET:

Saqqara, Tomb of Idout. A working scribe with his writing materials before him. His brush touches the hieroglyph of the open mouth, a subtle allusion to the power of the writer to give form.

the three letters 𓏤, I + ▢, P + ◠, T = IPET.

The sign of the throne, 𓊨, has two sounds, S + T = SET; the three strokes, │││, indicate that this is a plural. SET is then read SOOT.

As for this hieroglyph, ⊗, a circle inside of which two axles cross each other at right angles, it symbolizes a location, and is used to determine all words that designate a city, a town, or a country.

How to count in hieroglyphs:

| | = 1

| | | = 2

| | | | = 3

| | | | | = 4, etc.

∩ = 10

∩∩ = 20

∩∩∩ = 30, etc.

ϙ = 100

ϙϙ = 200, etc.

𐃷 (the lotus flower) = 1,000

𐃴 (the thumb) = 10, 000

𐃼 (the tadpole) = 100,000

𐃾 (the seated man with a feather on his head and his arms lifted in a joyful movement) = 1,000,000, which means an infinite number of things.

All you have to do is combine these elements to make a specific number. For example,

$$ϙ ∩∩ | | | | = 124$$

The hieroglyph ✗, which looks like our multiplication sign and our letter, is made to confuse Egyptologists! It has a number of different meanings:

OOPI, "to divide";

HESEB, "to count";

DJA, "to cross";

SOOA, "to pass by";

HEDJI, "to damage."

You need to consider the context to decide which is the appropriate meaning.

A FEW MEASURES

The Egyptians did not only know how to count but also how to measure. Although they did not have compasses, they understood the idea behind them and used a string instead.

Scribes measured everything: field areas, what was held in a bag of wheat, food portions, surfaces, and so on. It would take a technical treatise to show all the measures that the Egyptians were familiar with, but here are just a few essential ones.

ÂA

big

⌠ is a column, which has two sounds, Â + A = ÂA. The sign is followed by ⌡, which represents abstract ideas.

NEDJES

small

The word includes ⌇, N, + ⌐, DJ, + |, S = NEDJES, followed by the bird, ⌐, which determines words that fall into the category of evil or misery.

AOO

long

This sign represents a series of vertebrae and the spinal cord; it has two sounds, A + OO = AOO.

SEKH

wide

The word is composed of |, S, + ◉ , KH = SEKH, and is determined by a large vase.

The symbolic source of all measures is the illustrated eye, UDJAT, "the complete eye":

UDJAT
the complete eye

Each part of the eye is worth a fraction. For example: ⏜, the eyebrow, is worth ⅛; ○, the pupil, is worth ¼; ◁, the front of the eye, is worth ½.

"To have a good eye" is to know the just measure of things; "to have a bad eye" is to get them wrong.

Exercise 3

Question 1: Why is ⤙ the most important thing of all?

Question 2: In Egypt, is it good to be ⬒ 🦆, SHERI?

Question 3: Is it better to ⬤❘ or ⬤⌒?

Question 4: What abstract idea does the papyrus, ❦, embody?

Question 5: Why is this expression, 🪜 ⟱, a synonym of happiness?

Question 6: Must one respect ❘⌒⥿ ?

Question 7: How do you write "to open"?

Question 8: Which hieroglyph must you breathe in order to live?

Question 9: What familial link does 🦆, the duck, indicate?

Question 10: Is it good or bad to ⬤🦢⥿?

Question 11: Do you have a ⌒〰 ?

Question 12: Must a professor do this: ⏐⏑🦅🧍?

Question 13: Why is being 🗿 so important to the Egyptians?

Question 14: What does 🪶⚬ mean?

Question 15: Must you learn to 🦶🧍 ?

Question 16: What is an architect doing when he ⟨⬜⚬?

Question 17: How much is ⚵ ∩∩∩ ⏐⏐⏐⏐ ?

Question 18: Is the Eiffel Tower in Paris 🧍, ÂA, or 🦅⏐🦅, NEDJES?

Answer 1: Because it means "to love."

Answer 2: Certainly not, since this hieroglyph means "to be weak."

Answer 3: It depends on the circumstances. The same word REKH sometimes means "to know intellectually" (with the determinant 🧍), and sometimes "to know intimately" (with the determinant ⌒).

Answer 4: To be happy, vigorous, and healthy.

Answer 5: Because AOOT-IB means "largeness of heart."

Answer 6: Yes, of course, since he is the father.

Answer 7: ∪, OOP.

Answer 8: 🏺, TCHAOO, air.

Answer 9: "Son" or "daughter."

Answer 10: Quite bad, since KHEM means "to not know."

Answer 11: Yes, of course, since REN means "name."

Answer 12: Absolutely, since it means "to teach."

Answer 13: Because the word GER means "to be silent."

Answer 14: MA means "to see."

Answer 15: Yes, since CHED means "to read."

Answer 16: IP means "to count, to measure."

Answer 17: 234.

Answer 18: It is ÂA, big, and not NEDJES, small.

21 Speaking hieroglyphs

SPEECH IS A STICK
AND THE VOICE IS A PADDLE

The Egyptians placed a great value on silence. It was important not to waste one's breath. Loquaciousness and excess verbiage were seen as major faults. The voice and speech are tools, embodied by two of the main hieroglyphs. We are already acquainted with the first one:

MEDOO
speech

The stick, MEDOO, is used in the expression MEDOO NETER, "the speech (or sticks) of God." In other words, hieroglyphs and sacred texts. This stick is indispensable on the roads of the other world. As a stick, it is used by the traveler to avert danger. As speech, it lets him pronounce the formulas that will open all doors.

The hieroglyph for "voice" is a paddle:

KHEROO
the voice

This term is used in the very important expression MAÂ

KHEROO, "of just voice," which designates being recognized by the tribunal of the other world and confirms that he or she is fit to be reborn.

While the stick of language is used for earthbound travel, the paddle of voice is used for water trips. Our voice and our way of expression allow us to correctly navigate our boat on the river of life.

IS THE TONGUE A THRONE OR A FLAME?

Aesop, the Greek storyteller, had studied Egypt rather intently and once said that the tongue was both the best and worst of all things.

Here is the hieroglyph:

NES

the tongue

seen in profile, as if it were inside the mouth.

The root NES is used in the word NESET, "throne." In other words, the tongue can be the seat, or throne, of expression and command.

The expression IMY-R, "that which is in the mouth" (the tongue), is translated as "the chief, he who gives orders."

But NES is also "the flame"; the tongue can become scathing and destructive, can annihilate by fire and excess whoever misuses it.

WORDS TO TELL . . .

How does an Egyptian start? What words begin a ritual scene engraved on the temple walls? This group of hieroglyphs often appears:

DJED   MEDOO
words   *to tell*

And here again the scribes have been unkind to us and laid a trap. Indeed, ⌐ is an abbreviation of the word ⌐, which is read ⌐, DJ, + ⌐, D, = DJED, "to say."

We are now familiar with the stick, |, MEDOO, which means "word."

So the group:

is translated as "words to pronounce" or "words to tell."

When you visit the Egyptian temples, you will often see this hieroglyph on its walls. When Pharaoh addresses the gods, or when the gods speak to him, this is usually the opening expression.

Another layer of the verb, DJED, is that it has two different meanings: "to tell, to say," and "to be stable and durable." Thus, the words of Pharaoh and the gods are durable and assure the stability of the kingdom.

LET THE WORDS BE A MAGICAL KNOT

The hieroglyph:

TCHES

represents a vertebra, a knot, and a swallow's tail, which is used in Egyptian architecture to link stones.

This is obviously a linking sign, whether in the human body (the vertebra), in a building (the swallow's tail), or in dressing and magic (the knot).

Karnak, Temple of Khonsu. An example of hieroglyphs that is characteristic of the Ramessid period, and deeply engraved in the stone. Once again, we see the red crown.

The Egyptians attributed a magical character to all knots. The great magician goddess, Isis, knew the science of knots and, thus, could make and unmake the world. The word ⟶, TCHES, also means "magical words," "magical formulas," and "words that link." When we say TCHES, we are linking elements, rejoining that which was dispersed, and using the energy of the word to link them. Words are, thus, a magical tool that links and unites.

22 Thinking in hieroglyphs

TO KNOW OR TO FALL

"To know" is written:

REKH

to know

The word is composed of ⬭, R,+ ⊜, KH = REKH, which is determined by the abstract sign ⃒.

"To know," then, comes from the activity of the verb (the speaking mouth, ⬭), and of the choice between what is essential and what is not (the sieve, ⊜).

By reversing two of the consonants, we get KHER:

KHER

to fall

with the picture of the falling man.

The ignorant one, who refuses knowledge, is doomed to fall.

DIFFERENT WAYS OF THINKING

There are a number of different ways of saying "to think" in hieroglyphs. After all, the Egyptians considered this activity a crucial one.

Here are three of them:

KHEMET
to think

The word is composed of ⊜, KH, + 🐦, M, + ◠, T = KHEMET, which is again determined by the abstract sign 〣.

This term is a synonym of the word "three" (KHEMET). One is the divine unity and the other is a symbol of the first divine couple (Chu, light, and Tefnut, its receptacle), both of which are beyond the scope of human thinking, which begins with the number three.

KA
to think

This word is composed of ⌣, K, + 🐦, A = KA, which is determined by the abstract sign. This term is a synonym of KA, "creative energy"; thinking is, in fact, a way of using this immortal energy so as to introduce spirit into matter.

SIA
having intuition, thinking intuitively

This hieroglyph, which is also followed by the abstract sign, represents a folded, fringed piece of fabric. It was chosen to represent the most mysterious aspect of human thought, which is intuition—a direct contact with what is sacred and divine that seems to be hidden inside this fabric. The Pharaoh has the most SIA, intuition, and expresses it when dictating decrees.

Saqqara, Tomb of Idout. When the scribe writes, he carries
reserve brushes behind his ear.

23 Creating in hieroglyphs

THE CREATIVE EYE

IR

to create, to make

There is no doubt that the eye is creative and has been chosen to embody the ideas "to make, to create"; there is no chance in this choice. If "to listen, to hear" (with ◢, SEDJEM, the cow's ear) is the right attitude for attaining knowledge, one must then act, which is when the eye comes into play. Opening one's eyes is to enter into the world of action with a lucid and constructive vision. The eyelids are called "arms of the eye."

The eye in the hieroglyph is not a human one—it belongs to the falcon, Horus, who sees much more intensely and precisely than any man.

"Eye of Horus" is also the name given to any offering, be it milk, bread, wine, and so on. An offering to the gods is an "eye of Horus" because one must make the offering in order to see the divine.

The Egyptians kept their eyes open even in death—the mummy's eyes could not be closed or else it would not find its way in the other world.

The creator has two eyes: the right one is the Sun, the left one is the Moon. If God's eyes were to leave his face

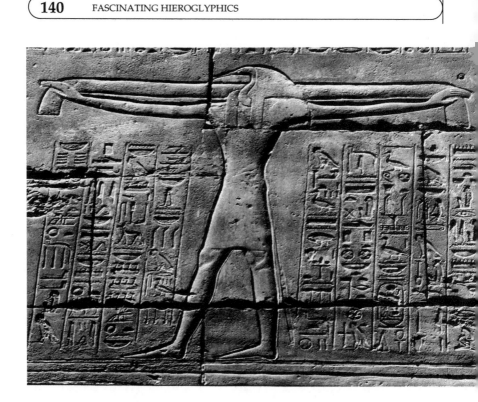

Karnak. Among the columns of hieroglyphs, Thot extends his arms and thus gives a measure of the temple.

and run away, misery and destruction would fall upon humanity. Thot, the master of hieroglyphs, must then go find these eyes and bring them back to their rightful place. Only then would harmony and joy reign once again.

SEDJEM, "to hear," means that one has the ear of the cow Hathor, goddess of the stars; IR, "to create," is to have the eye of the falcon Horus, god of the sky.

Hathor and Horus celebrated their wedding with a magnificent feast that brought together the priests and priestesses of the temples of Dendera and Edfu.

A CREATOR MUST HAVE A POT

Let us take a simple pot:

KHENEM

This modest object is used to write the name of the god Khnoum, a man with a ram's head whose major role is that of the potter, creating men on his wheel.

The small pot made by him is read KHENEM and means "to join, to unite, to protect, to make, to create." The image of a potter working at his wheel is that of a serene creator turning simple elements (the earth) into necessary objects for daily life.

24 Beautiful truths

THE GOOD AND THE BEAUTIFUL

The hieroglyph 𓄤, which represents the heart (or lungs) and trachea, is read NEFER and means "good, beautiful, perfect, accomplished."

We have already seen it as "good," in opposition to

𓄤𓂝	NEFER	the sun's brilliance	
𓄤𓂋𓃒	NEFERET	the cow	
𓄤𓍍	NEFER	god's clothing (𓍍 is the fabric)	
𓄤𓏰	NEFER	grain (𓏰 is a bushel from which the grain spills)	
𓄤𓏴	NEFER	wine, beer	
𓄤𓈖	NEFER	the necropolis (where the eternal dwelling places are)	
𓄤𓉐	NEFER	the king's tomb (or that of the god)	
𓄤𓀅	NEFER	the handsome boy (and future army recruit)	
𓄤𓂋𓋔	NEFERET	Pharaoh's white crown	

142

"bad," and as a qualifier for Osiris, "the good one," who is perfectly accomplished and went through death to be reborn.

What did the Egyptians see as good and beautiful?

This list on page 142 gives us an idea.

BEAUTY IS IN THE EYE

ÂN

to be beautiful

The word is composed of ⸗, Â + 〰, N = ÂN, followed by the made-up eye.

The Egyptians used the skillfully made-up eye to represent beauty and charm. This make-up is in some sense related to the art of writing since Sechat, the goddess of books and hieroglyphs, is also the patron of make-up artists.

This is why the word ÂNY, "the charmer," represents a writing desk.

ÂNET, "the nail," must be attractive and well groomed. The expression "to do one's nails" exists in hieroglyphs.

ÂN is also the word for the adze, the carpenter's tool used to open the mummy's eyes and mouth, thus creating a supernatural beauty.

TRUTH IS AN OSTRICH FEATHER

What is Egyptian education geared toward? What is the basis of pharaonic civilization? What do the sages search for?

A simple ostrich feather,

ß

MAÂT

This hieroglyph has four sounds. It can also be written as:

MA + Â + T = MAÂT

When a person is judged by Osiris, Maat's feather is put on one side of the scales, and the heart of the judged is on the other. The heart must be as light as Maat's feather to be recognized as just and granted immortality.

Maat is the eternal rule that reigns over the universe; it existed before humanity and will exist after it. Maat is accuracy, truth, the order of things, the rudder that steers the ship, the measure of all things. The verb MAÂ means "to drive, to direct," but also "to make an offering," since that is the most efficient way of warding off misery and disorder.

Maat can also be written with ⸗, the pedestal of a statue, and thus indicate balance.

The opposite of Maat is:

ISEFET
disorder, chaos, misery, injustice

The word ISEFET is determined by "the bird of evil." Maat is the heart of Egyptian thought and civilization. Pharaoh's true role is to replace Isefet with Maat—to put order in the place of disorder, and truth in the place of lies.

There is no greater task than this, for the happiness of a people, just like that of an individual, rests upon the practice of Maat, which is both accuracy and justice.

The tribunal of the other world asks only one fundamental question of the person who is being judged:

"Did you spend your life respecting and practicing Maat?"

25 In the company of the gods

THE GODS IN HIEROGLYPHS

Egypt was full of gods.

To enter into the sacred realm was to encounter:

DJESER
sacred, splendid, magnificent

The outstretched arm holding a scepter has three sounds: ⌐, DJ, + ⎮, S, + ⌐, R = DJESER.

This is the name of the Pharaoh who, with his famous architect, Imhotep, built the step pyramid at Saqqara.

DJESER also means "to exclude, to isolate," as this sacred world must be kept away from the profane.

What is a god in hieroglyphs?

NETER

a pole from which waves a piece of cloth.

The word is a synonym for NETER, "natron," the salt used to mummify the body and make it divine. The feminine NETERET is "the divine eye." This pole was found at

Cairo Museum. Everything is in hieroglyphs, including this strange work called the "cube statue," from which a human head emerges.

temple entrances. From far away, one could see the divine banner floating in the wind, signaling the sacred dwelling place.

In hieroglyphs, we often see the masculine divinity represented as 𓀭, a seated, serene man with his wig and postiche beard. Female deities are represented by an equally serene seated woman 𓀭.

The name of Atoum, the first deity to rise from the ocean of energy, the Noun, is written with a sledge ⎯⎯⚊,

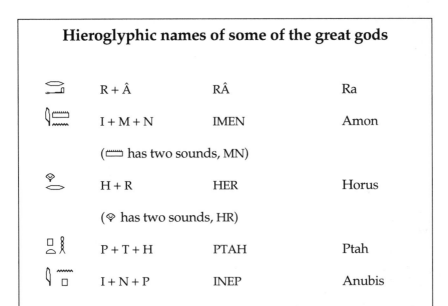

Hieroglyphic names of some of the great gods

𓂋𓂝	R + Â	RÂ	Ra
𓇋𓏠𓈖	I + M + N	IMEN	Amon
	(𓏠 has two sounds, MN)		
𓅃	H + R	HER	Horus
	(𓅃 has two sounds, HR)		
𓊨𓏏𓎛	P + T + H	PTAH	Ptah
𓇋𓈖𓊪	I + N + P	INEP	Anubis

The names of Osiris and Isis are somewhat problematic to read and interpret:

𓊨𓁹   is read OOSIR, Osiris (the seat of the eye);

𓊨𓏏   is read ASET, Isis, "the throne, the seat."

which was used to carry stones for the raising of sacred buildings. The name Atoum means both "to be" and "not to be," thus covering all forms of existence.

A good way to approach the gods is:

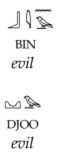

DOOA

to adore, to venerate

both of which can also be written with ✶, the star.

MAY THE DEITIES DELIVER US FROM EVIL

As we have seen earlier,

is a either a sparrow or a similar bird. It is a noisy, agitated, destructive creature that reproduces endlessly. Found at the end of words belonging to the category of what is bad, small, and weak, it is called "the bird of evil."

We have encountered another word that means evil, ISE-FET—the opposite of MAÂT, order, justice, the rule. Here are two other common terms:

BIN

evil

DJOO

evil

◻, the mountain or desert, has two sounds, DJ + OO. It is a dangerous region where Seth's animals live.

𓅬 𓅭

IOO

evil, an evil action

This term is written with a calf lying down. It has two sounds, I + OO. It is a synonym of the verb IOU, "to be without a boat," which means to be condemned to misery and destitution, since without a boat one cannot get from one shore to the next, nor can one travel the river to the other world.

Among the beings that embody evil, there is also the enormous snake found in the tombs of the Valley of the Kings, who tried drinking the Nile in order to keep the solar boat from being reborn. The boat's crew was able to nail it down with magical incantations.

This snake, which became a dragon in the Middle Ages, is named:

ÂPEP

better known as Apophis. It is also called:

NIK

There are other forms of evil that must be fought and subdued:

AD

aggressiveness

The word is determined by a crocodile, which is well known as an ferocious attacker.

AD also means "to tremble," for aggressiveness makes us lose our serenity and inner peace.

One note: FENEDJ, "to be angry," literally means "having

Saqqara, Tomb of Mererouka. The mouth and sieve form the word REKH, "to know."

(someone) in the nose."

SENEDJ

fear

is a trussed goose that has three sounds (S + N + DJ). That is what fear can do.

But the greatest evil that can afflict an individual is:

ÂOON   IB

rapaciousness   *of heart*

This attribute means greed and envy.

Let us remember the sage's words:

Greed is an incurable sickness . . . it is the amalgam of all sorts of evil, it is a bag holding all that is hateful.
The greedy man will have no tomb.[1]

---

1. See Christian Jacq. *L'Enseignement du Sage Ptahhotep.* La Maison de Vie, 1993, pp. 97–99.

   Who can deliver us from all of these afflictions if not the gods, and a benevolent Isis in particular?
   Here is a prayer that was often addressed to her:

ASET	SEFEKH	OOI	M	BIN
Isis	*deliver*	*me*	*from*	*evil*

Cairo Museum. Two eyes on the lintel of this door contemplate the one who is about to travel into the other world.

26 A good house in a good town

There is an expression that says "A roof and a heart are all one needs to be happy." Let's now look at the roof. The most frequently used Egyptian word for house is:

⊏⊐

PER

The hieroglyph represents a closed property rather than a simple house. The dominant idea expressed here is that of a closed, protective space with an entrance door.

This house can be found in the country or in the city, which is written:

⊗

NIOOT

town, city

This is a somewhat strange hieroglyph, since Egyptian cities did not resemble a circle occupied by two perpendicular lines. But what this hieroglyph does is associate the circle and the cross, and thus organizes space in a symbolic manner.

West Thebes, Tomb of Rameses III. The sublime face of a banquet guest.

27 Dinner's ready!

LET'S EAT AND DRINK

Here are three ways of writing the verb "to eat":

OONEM

The signs ⸷, ⸷, and ⸷ all have two sounds (OO + N). They are completed by ⸷, M, and the sign of a man carrying food to his mouth.

In these three ways of writing "to eat," we see:

—the use of the flower, ⸷, probably to show that it's necessary to understand the subtle aspect of food. This is the most important, as it nourishes the KA;

—the hare, ⸷, well known for its voracity, and probably used here as an allusion to Osiris, an incarnation of the nourishing earth, and to the grain that dies to give birth to wheat;

—and this object, ⸷, which resembles a cross, remains an enigma. Let's hope that it will one day be understood.

OONEM is also used to designate "the flame" that absorbs everything it consumes.

Drinking is another essential activity:

SOOR

The word is written with ⟶, S, and 🐦, the swallow, which has two sounds, OO + R, and with ⟶, R, which is added for easier reading. The determinant is, once again, the man carrying food to his mouth.

OONEM "to eat"; SOOR "to drink."

But to eat and drink what?

The Egyptian diet was rich and varied, and quite different from that of present-day Egypt. It consisted of meats, fish (many Nile species have now disappeared), vegetables, fruit, pastries, wines of all sorts, beer, etc.

The list of delicious dishes was very long.

Nonetheless, there is a symbol, often used in texts, which comprised food in general, whether liquid or solid:

⊖	⊖
T	HENQET
bread	*beer*

⊖ is bread rising in a pan; it is read as T. ⊖ is a jug of beer, and is read HENQET.

Having T-HENQET at your disposal means that you have a basic diet, consisting of a multi-cereal bread and a beer that was both nutritious and digestible.

This hieroglyphic group is found in an expression on tomb walls:

⊖ ⊖ ⊖
what comes out from the voice = the offering

⊏⊐, the enclosure, is read PERET and here means "what comes out"; ⟆, the paddle, is read KHEROO and means "voice."

The expression PERET-KHEROO is translated as "what

comes out from the voice," and evokes the ritual words that make food appear. With hieroglyphs, the word makes it a good meal.

Something that the ancient Egyptians insisted upon was wine:

IREP

Ancient Egypt was a civilization in which the grape played a major role. The vintages of the Delta and various oases were well known and appreciated. Winemaking scenes are common on tomb walls, and resting under a trellis heavy with grapes was a pleasure greatly appreciated. Wine was drunk during feasts and banquets. Then, during the Arab invasion, the vines were destroyed.

The contemporary tourist has to be content with (or rather abstain from) a wine named after the famous poet Omar Khayyám, himself a great wine enthusiast. Truly, he did not deserve to be remembered so cruelly.

TO YOUR HEALTH!

Talking of wine and beer evokes the conviviality of the phrase "To your health!"

Here it is in hieroglyphs:

N   KA   K
to   the ka   of you

Or, in other words, "to your ka," or "to your vital energy."

FOR A CLEAN KITCHEN

Hygiene and cleanliness were extremely important in ancient Egypt, and this was shown in the very word for kitchen:

OOÂBET

The word OOÂBET literally means "the pure place," a clean place where only pure foods could enter. The word OOÂBET also designates the mummification workshop where the immortal body, which must be free of any stains, is prepared; OOÂBET is also the tomb, which is free of all evil.

OOÂB is "the meal of offering," one that has been purified by the appropriate rites. ⬚ or ⬚, OOÂB, "the pure one," is the title of any person admitted into the temple after having been purified by water.

Another purification method, which was used in the kitchen, was the flame, whose usefulness in cooking foods is obvious.

Flames are designated in a number of ways in hieroglyphs. Here is one of them:

NESER

The hieroglyph's lower part, seen from above, represents three stones around a hearth from which three flames are rising.

THREE MEALS A DAY

IÂOO   R

the washing   *of the mouth*   = breakfast

The word is composed of 𓇋, I, + 𓂝, Â, + 𓅱, OO = IÂOO, followed by the water sign, and by 𓂋, R, the mouth. It tells us that breakfast began with washing and a purification, with the idea that the food absorbed had to keep the mouth pure.

SETY — R

the delicious taste — *of the mouth* = lunch

The word is composed of 𓋴, S, + 𓏏, T, + 𓏭, Y = SETY, with the determinant 𓐎, indicating that the word belongs in the category of smells and perfumes. We are not absolutely certain what this hieroglyph represents; some see a small sachet of perfume, while others see a pimple or blotch. SETY means "perfume," "the good smell," "the delicious taste"; the term is followed by 𓂋, R, "the mouth."

So, for lunch, a person insisted on the quality and taste of the food, which was expected to keep the breath fresh.

And finally:

MESHEROOT

the night one = dinner

The word is composed of 𓅓, M, + 𓈙, SH, + 𓃭, ROO, + 𓏏, T = MESHEROOT, followed by 𓇼, which indicates the time of day.

This expression could also be understood as "what is appreciated thanks to (M) the nose (SHERET)," for dinner was also to offer delicious smells.

WHO SLEEPS DINES

After a good dinner, one retires for a good night's sleep:

ACHOOT

the bed

The word is composed of , A, + , CH, + , OO, + , T = ACHOOT, followed by , a branch, indicating that the word belongs to the category of wooden objects.

The root ACHI is used to write "the wet nurse." We may then make the leap that bed, and, thus, sleep, feeds one as well as a wet nurse, and that, in fact, he who sleeps dines.

28 As long as you've got your health!

HEALTH IS IN THE EYE

SENEB

health

The word is composed of 𓊪, S, + 𓈖, N, + 𓃀, B, plus the abstract idea determinant. Another word to express a similar idea is:

OODJA

The word is composed of 𓎗, OO, + 𓏏, DJ, + 𓅓, A, and the same abstract idea determinant as above.

This root OODJA also means "to go, to move slowly," which means to be well. Isn't moving correctly a proof of good health? The UDJAT is the complete eye, healthy and intact, and was used as a model for the protective amulets so beloved both by ancient Egyptians and present-day tourists.

There is no doubt that for the Pharaoh's lucky subjects, health was in the eye!

Karnak. Sechat, sovereign of the dwelling place of books and mistress of writing, helps to build the temple by planting a stake.

AN INEXHAUSTIBLE ENERGY

A person's health must be taken care of, and the basic food is:

MOO

water

This root, MOO, is also used to write other words having to do with liquids, such as urine or saliva (literally "water in the mouth").

Where does this crucial water and energy come from?

It comes from an inexhaustible supply, a sort of cosmic ocean that contains all forms of life, which the Egyptians called

NOON

The three small pots are a triple sound (N + OO + N = NOON); the three wavy lines at the end of the word refer to a liquid and energetic state.

According to the Egyptian philosophic texts, this NOON is inexhaustible. It is comparable to the limitless immensity from which a few islands, such as the earth, emerge, and to which they will return. Our disappearance is thus programmed.

All forms of energy, whether it is the Nile or springwater, come from this ocean, the "matter" from which all is made.

MAKING HAIR!

The hieroglyph ⌐ represents a strand of curly hair. It has two sounds, CH + N = CHEN and means hair.

But the same hair strand can also be read two other ways:

⌐

INEM

skin

⌐

IOON

color

With this hieroglyph, Egypt was clearly linking the notions of "hair," "skin," and "color," characteristics of a normally developed and harmonious human being.

One must also add the notion of "mourning"; during funerals, hired mourners would let their hair flow as a sign of sadness.

Exercise 4

Question 1: Which hieroglyph is used to symbolize the voice?

Question 2: Can you read and translate ⪥⪥ ?

Question 3: Is it better to ⬭ 🦅 ◠⫽ or to ▭⫽?

Question 4: Which hieroglyph is used to write "the beautiful, the good?"

Question 5: Which hieroglyphs are used to write "truth," "justice," "harmony," "the Rule"?

Question 6: When in front of the pyramids, the pilgrim says only one thing: 🦅⫽ . Why?

Question 7: If you come across something or someone that is ⫽⫽〰, should you get closer or get away?

Question 8: Should you mistrust someone who is 🦅⪥⪥?

Question 9: How do you feel when your are ⪤?

Question 10: Why is it said that ▭🦅〰⪥ is a mortal ill?

Question 11: Is it better to live in a ⊐ or ⊗?

Question 12: Is it better to ✛🦅🦆 or to ⪥🦆?

Question 13: If someone offers you ⫽ ▫ ⪤ , are you likely to accept?

Question 14: Is it prudent to use 🦆?

Question 15: If you are invited to a ⫽⪤▫⌣, should you accept?

Question 16: Should you accept if you are invited to 𓄿 𓂋𓃀 𓎡 ?

Question 17: Why do many people consider 𓂝𓏏𓆓 the most precious gift of all?

Question 18: Is 𓈖 indispensable?

Question 19: What hieroglyph puts you in rapport with hair, skin, and color?

Answer 1: The paddle, 𓏃, KHEROO.

Answer 2: TCHES, "magical words."

Answer 3: Both. The first word, KHEMET, means "to think"; the second, SIA, "thinking intuitively."

Answer 4: 𓄤, NEFER.

Answer 5: 𓌳 and ⸺ (MAÂ, MAÂT).

Answer 6: Because DJESER means "sacred, splendid, magnificent."

Answer 7: You should move away, as BIN means "evil, bad."

Answer 8: Absolutely, because AD means "aggressiveness, to be aggressive."

Answer 9: SENEDJ means "fear, to be fearful."

Answer 10: Because ÂOON-IB is "greediness of heart."

Answer 11: You can live in both simultaneously: PER means "house," NIOOT means "the city."

Answer 12: Both are indispensable: OONEM is "to eat" and SOOR is "to drink."

Answer 13: Probably, especially if it is a good one, since IREP is "wine."

Answer 14: That depends. It is NESER, the flame.

Answer 15: Yes, since this is SETY-R, or lunch.

Answer 16: It depends on who is asking, since ACHOOT is "the bed."

Answer 17: Because it is SENEB, "health."

Answer 18: Certainly, since it is MOO, "water."

Answer 19: , the lock of hair.

29 At the doctor's

If there is one technician who uses magical formulas, it is the doctor:

SOONOO
the doctor

The word is composed of ——, the arrow (which suggests the notion of targeting, and thus of rendering a precise diagnosis), and the pot, ○ (which contains the medicines).

The root SOON also means "the sickness, the pain," which the doctor must cure.

Prescriptions are the domain of the antelope:

CHESA
*to be skillful, to be learned,
and the medical prescription*

This quick and smart quadruped was seen as a model for the doctor, who must also act quickly and with precision.

The word "medication" is written quite remarkably:

Saqqara, Tomb of Mererouka. The ritual slaughter of an ox, and the cutting of the leg, which is a hieroglyph for "power."

PEKHERET

remedy, potion, medication

This sign represents the intestines; the root PEKHER means "to circulate." The medication administered by the doctor must circulate throughout the body starting, apparently, with the intestines.

Let's note that the word "pharmacist" comes from ancient Egypt and literally means "the magical medication maker." Nowadays, our best wizards are found in the dispensaries.

30   A day at work

GETTING UP ON THE RIGHT FOOT

Let's take a good foot, ⌐, straight and firm.
    Then let's stretch our arms, Ц.
    And let's look at the rising sun, ⊙.
    That's how we get the word

⌐Ц⊙

BEKA

morning

It is formed by ⌐, B, + Ц, KA = BEKA, which can be translated as "a place of energy."

PESEDJ

the back

is a synonym of PESEDJ, "light."
    This underlines the importance of the spinal column, in which an energy comparable to light travels.
    Having gotten up on the right foot, with our back in fine shape, we look good, with a clear complexion:

TEP	NEFER
head	*good*

"Good head" also means "the right way to act."

By associating the head and the face, we get the very image of authority:

HER	TEP
the one who predominates	*and who orders*

To signify immediate action, we associate the face and arm:

HER	ÂOOY
face	*two arms*

which means "immediately." In other words, the head, without delay, transmits orders to the arms, which go into action.

TO GET UP, LET'S RAISE THE LADDER

Everything has an end, even a good night's sleep. We have to get up, and hieroglyphs unite these notions in a telling term:

ÂHÂ

to get up, to rise

This hieroglyph has three sounds, Â + H + Â = ÂHÂ, and represents the mast of a boat topped with a rope ladder.

The sign ⌐ indicates that the word is in the category relating to movement, which is indeed the case when we get up.

To be up in the correct way is not, for the Egyptian, to be static, but to move like the mast and ladder of a rope, both fixed and solid but also able to withstand the winds and boat movements without breaking or losing one's stability. ÂHÂ designates the correct position of things or the correct positioning of participants in a ritual. It implies an ordered movement that leads to stability.

Furthermore, the term ÂHÂOO, which is determined by the sun, means "the time of life." Our existence is the time during which we are up, straight like boat masts, and able to use the rope ladder to climb and see farther.

SALUTATIONS TO THE SUN

The Egyptian's first spiritual activity was a salutation to the rising sun, which was seen as a miracle. The sun had, indeed, once again fought the darkness and won.

Knowing a prayer to the sun is indispensable. Here is a simplified version of a text written by the famous Akhenaton himself:

KHÂ	K	NEFER	M	AKHET	ITEN	ÂNKH
Apparition	*of you*	*in perfection*	*on*	*the horizon*	*Aton*	*living*

"You appear in perfection on the horizon, living Aton."

The sign  is a hill over which the brilliant fringe of the rising sun appears. KHÂ means "to appear like the sun," and is also used to describe the Pharaoh on his throne.

, K, is the masculine personal pronoun, in the second person singular, "you."

It is impossible to say "you appear" in hieroglyphs because the verb is placed before the pronoun, so we get "apparition of you," which we translate as "you appear."

SEHEDJ	K	TA	NEB	M	NEFER	K
illumination	*of you*	*earth*	*each*	*by*	*beauty*	*of you*

"You illuminate each earth by your beauty."

The word ⌐ is composed of ǀ, S, and ǀ, HEDJ = SEHEDJ, "to illuminate," determined by the sun.

ǀ is the bludgeon HEDJ, "the white, the illuminating," with which the Pharaoh consecrates offerings and knocks down the enemy coming out of the darkness. It illuminates and dissipates night.

LET US DRESS WISELY

Was there fashion in ancient Egypt?

During the Old Kingdom, at the time of the pyramids, clothing was simple: a loincloth for men, a strap dress for women that left the breasts uncovered.

During the New Kingdom, elegance and refinement became fashionable, which the old sages did not see as progress.

ÂREQ

to dress

The word is composed of ▭, Â, + ⌐, R, + △, Q = ÂREQ.
⌐ is a folded fabric. But ÂREQ also means "to fold, to bend," which is necessary to get dressed. What is more surprising is that another synonym of ÂREQ is translated as "to perceive, to have knowledge of something, to be wise."

Does that mean that you should dress wisely and not indulge in sartorial excesses?

WHEN YOU NEED TO GO ...

After getting dressed, you must go to work. A series of hieroglyphs makes it easier to get to the workplace:

PERI

go!

The word is composed of ⊏⊐, PER, + ◊, I = PERI; the root PER means "to climb, to exit."

To go more softly, the simplest thing to do is to move gracefully and lightly, just like a reed on legs:

II

to go, to come

Both legs are followed by the baby quail, which is also good at moving, and form the other most common movement verb:

IOO

to come

Or with the lock on the legs, you can give an order:

IS

let's go!

When moving vigorously, you can even carry a basin:

SHEM

to go, to move

Perhaps this is an allusion to the incessant movement of running water.

If you need to carry something while walking, it is indicated by a pot on legs:

$$\text{Ĵ}$$

IN

to bring, to take, to go get

from which comes the word INOO, "products, tributes" and "contributions."

As to the word INOO, "what one takes," it is the mat *par excellence*. There was no more essential object for an Egyptian, since it was used as a blanket, a bed, and even a shroud. Having a good mat was like having mobile furniture.

BEING POLITE

This is how the Egyptians said "hello":

INEDJ	HER	K
may be protected	*the face*	*of you*

This ancient salutation caused a lot of would-be decipherers a lot of problems.

The hieroglyph represents an object that has still not been identified—another intriguing enigma for future Egyptologists to solve!

We do recognize the sign NEDJ, which is here preceded by an I, from which we get the term INEDJ, determined by ⸗, the sign of abstract ideas.

The root NEDJ means "to salute," but also "to protect, to take counsel, to ask, to consult, to save (someone from misery)." When ancient Egyptians said "hello," all of these meanings were implied.

Another way of saying hello:

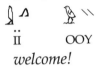

NYNY

By saying NYNY, you transmit energy (⁓).

It is the act of a hypnotizer, since we see energy coming from the hands of the one saluting. When Isis resuscitated Osiris she did so with NYNY.

And finally, a charming expression:

ÏÏ   OOY

welcome!

TO WORK

Good organization of work was one of the major virtues in ancient Egypt. The Egyptians were able to organize a work-site like no one else.

BAK

to work

This word is composed of the bird , BA, + ⌒, K = BAK, and the word is determined by an outstretched arm holding a stick, which indicates effort.

It is interesting to note the bird's presence in this word, since it is often translated as "soul." Does work help give one soul?

BAK is "the worker, the servant"; BAKOO are "tasks, revenues," but also "taxes."

Another way of representing work is:

KAT

This shows a man carrying something on his head, which stresses the somewhat weighty load of work, but also the energy (KA) that it both needs and produces.

For the Egyptians, two essential elements of the immortal, BA and KA, were associated with work, which emphasizes its great nobility in the eyes of Egyptians.

31 Acquiring in hieroglyphs

To own or be owned?

ICH

to own

The word is composed of a fetter mounted on legs, , ICH, and is determined by a man wielding a stick.

ICH, "to own," implies an effort. The term also means "to take possession," "to conquer," "to take away." Besides the effort, to own is a sort of fetter, whether you hold on to your possessions or are held by them.

To own goods, to be rich, is not seen as a fault, but as necessitating a certain state of mind that is represented by this hieroglyph, a basket:

NEB

The basket NEB is the receptacle of goods and possessions, but also suggests the idea of "mastery." NEB, "the owner," is also "the master (of his possessions)" if he is able to manage them.

NEB also means "all, each, each one" and the root NEB is used to say "gold," and "to work a metal." Wouldn't any-

Valley of the Kings, Tomb of Thutmose III. Horus and Thot present the complete eye, a symbol of totality, fully accomplished creation, and health.

one who had attained mastery of himself and of what he owned be able to transform gold, the flesh of the gods, into material goods? The other way of "possessing" is indicated by the preposition

⚱

KHER

under, in possession of

To be "under something" is to not only carry it and possess it, but also to bear the weight of the thing in question. KHERET is "the thing owned," which means "carried, borne"; the word is also translated as "the base," "the bottom part."

And let's remember that KHEROOT represent the "lower parts" of the male—the testicles.

We must be careful that riches, growing too abundant, do not become uncontrollable, as symbolized by a lizard:

🦎

ÂCHA

multitude, quantity

This hieroglyph that says someone uses too many words is ÂCHA-R—literally, "the lizard in the mouth."

CAPITAL AND INTERESTS

If capital acquired through work comes from the Latin word *caput* (head), the idea already existed in ancient Egypt:

𓁶

TEP

the head

When it is used in administrative and fiscal documents, the word "head" means "capital," work revenue.

As for the notion of "interests," it is explicitly shown in hieroglyphs:

Karnak, a pylon of the Temple of Khonsu. Between the two towers of the pylons, above the door appeared a victorious sun after it had won its fight against darkness.

FAT

what brings a good yield = interests

32 The traveling hieroglyph

AH, THE BEAUTIFUL VOYAGES . . .

The Egyptians were great travelers who used the Nile as their highway (with tolls, already). So it comes as no surprise that the two terms most often used to say "to travel" come from sailors:

KHED

to go north

(going with the current)

KHENET

to go south

(going against the current)

The first hieroglyph represents three jars.

Some other terms for the expression "to travel" use the boat, ⌂, and the moving human legs, ⌂.

The earthbound road is drawn like this:

OOAT

the road, the way

The sign is composed of the road itself and of trees or

Saqqara, Tomb of Mererouka. This procession of carriers of offerings evokes the riches of ancient Egypt; the hieroglyphs above the scene talk about "bringing all good things."

plants that are shown lying down so that they can be seen. It would be impossible to imagine a good road that isn't bordered by trees, giving shade to the walking traveler.

An important sentence to know is

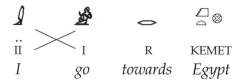

İİ	I	R	KEMET
I	*go*	*towards*	*Egypt*

"Egypt" is written with the hieroglyph ◿, which may be a fragment of the scaly skin of a crocodile. The root KEM means "black" and Egypt is designated as "the black earth," which is fertile thanks to the deposits of silt. The sign is completed by ◡, the feminine T, and by the determinant ⊗, which shows that the term is geographic.

For those leaving for Egypt,

PER	NEFER
trip	*good*

WHAT IS FOREIGN IS BERBER

Egypt welcomed many foreigners, but it also had a very strong cultural and territorial identity. Foreign cultures melted into Egypt—not the other way around.

All foreigners were symbolized by the expression "the nine arcs," which is why the hieroglyph for nine, ＿, is often found on statues below Pharaoh's feet, marking his magical domination so as to avoid the troubles and dangers of invasion.

And here is the Egyptian name of a foreign place where, unfortunately for humanity, languages were confused:

B   B   R

BEBER

Babel

33 To arms!

AN ENTIRE ARSENAL

One must fight against evil. The Egyptians, although they were not particularly bellicose, had an army that was well organized and able to defend the country against invaders from Sudan, Libya, and Asia.

This hieroglyph is quite explicit:

ÂHÂ

to fight

The hieroglyph represents two arms, one holding a shield and the other a club. In other words, something to defend with, and something to attack with.

Two other hieroglyphs determine words that imply an effort or fight:

— , the extended arm holding a stick;

— , the standing man yielding a stick.

 can be read NEKHT, "victorious," because it relates to the idea of expanding your efforts towards success.

With the bludgeon, , HEDJ, it is possible to break an enemy's skull.

Karnak. Foreign captives are represented as tied-up men; their names are written inside the cartouches.

The bow, ⚊, lets you shoot the arrow, ⟶.

The dagger, 𝄄, also indicates the idea of "first, preeminent."

As for the stick, ⟍, it suggests ideas of "throwing" as well as characterizing a clan or tribe. It also embodies, in a surprising way, the notion of creation, as if it was conceived of as a throw.

THE MOST EFFICIENT ARM: MAGIC

If there was one Egyptian word that you would need to know to face the basic rigors of life, it would be

HEKA

magic

The word is composed of 𓏤, H, + 𓂓, KA = HEKA, determined by the sign for abstract ideas.

Magical power, when it is well used, allows for the manipulation of the energy that links both worlds.

In the teaching that the Pharaoh gave to his son, the sovereign revealed that HEKA could help a human being turn away a bad destiny. The universe is full of HEKA. It is up to the conscientious man to find it and use it appropriately.

A stick and a knife could be used as guides

𓌀

OODJ

to command, to govern, to
order, to act as a pilot

This is a very strong term, usually used to mean the order that Pharaoh gives so as to determine the country's politics.

The sign 𓌄, OODJ, is a stick with a rope curled around it. The stick governs and the rope links.

OODJ also means "expedition" (ordered by Pharaoh), an "inscription" (based on Pharaoh's words), a stele (engraved and raised to let Pharaoh's thoughts be known).

𓌁

SECHEM

to drive, to guide, to instruct, to show the way

is another frequently used term. The hieroglyph shows us a knife 𓌁 on legs.

This knife lets us cut a way through life's undergrowth, open the road, and advance by making the right choices. Whoever doesn't know how to make his way with a sharp knife does not know how to lead his life.

Exercise 5

Question 1: What do you say when you meet a ⸺ ○ 🀄 ?

Question 2: Is it pleasant to absorb a ▱ ?

Question 3: If you feel good during ⅃ ⊔ ⊙, are you a morning or evening person?

Question 4: How should you act when with a ◈ ⌘?

Question 5: What do you do when you ⌁ ⊿ ?

Question 6: Is ⸝⸜ an essential worry?

Question 7: Is ⍝ an encouragement or an insult?

Question 8: What is the difference between ⍭ and ⍮?

Question 9: Do you like to BAK, ⍦ ⌐ ?

Question 10: What effort is implied by the verb ⍚ ⍥ ?

Question 11: Which hieroglyph implies the ideas of "possession" and "mastery"?

Question 12: What do you run into when faced with ⍜ ?

Question 13: Why is it important to be careful on the ⍘ ?

Question 14: Why are pharaohs described as ⌐ ?

Question 15: What is ⌇⊔⌇ used for?

Question 16: What does it mean to ⌁ ?

Question 17: Is it easy or difficult to ⍝ ?

Answer 1: You tell him what it is you are suffering from, since this is a SOONOO, "a doctor."

Answer 2: It depends, since PEKHERET means "medication."

Answer 3: BEKA means "morning."

Answer 4: With deference, for HER-TEP is "the superior" who predominates and orders.

Answer 5: ÂHÂ means "to get up."

Answer 6: It depends on fashion and climate, as ÂREQ means "to dress."

Answer 7: An encouragement, since IS means "Let's go!"

Answer 8: The first hieroglyph, II, means "to come, to go"; the second one, IN, means "to bring, to take, to go get."

Answer 9: BAK means "to work."

Answer 10: ICH means "to take possession, to conquer, to own."

Answer 11: The basket, 𓎟, NEB.

Answer 12: ÂCHA, "the multitude, quantity."

Answer 13: Because OOAT is "the road, the way."

Answer 14: Because this hieroglyph can be read NEKHT, "victorious."

Answer 15: HEKA, magic, is used to deal with life's troubles and difficulties.

Answer 16: OODJ means "to command, to govern, to order."

Answer 17: Quite difficult, as SECHEM means "to drive, to guide, to instruct, to show the way."

34 Old age and serenity

BEING OLD MEANS BEING USEFUL

The old man, bowed down with age, and using a stick to walk,

𓀗

is read IAOO
and means *being old*

Old age, according to Ptahhotep, is a test because of all of the ills with which it overwhelms an aged person. But the term IAOO is based on the root IAOOT, "to be useful."

The elderly, in fact, fulfill an essential function: they are fundamentally useful because (like Ptahhotep, who lived to be 110 years old) they pass along their wisdom and experience.

IAOO also means "to venerate, to adore." The elderly are venerable, if they have fulfilled their function, and they themselves revere life and the gods.

SERENITY IS A TABLE
LADEN WITH OFFERINGS

𓊵

HETEP

represents a table of offerings with a loaf of bread on it.

Saqqara, Tomb of Idout. The bludgeon HEDJ, whose name means "the white, the illuminating," is what the Pharaoh uses to kill his enemies and consecrate offerings.

The term HETEP, frequently used in the texts, means not only "a table of offerings," but also "peace, serenity, fulfill-ment, calm." It is through offerings of food to the gods that a person can reach the state of HETEP, which characterizes the sages.

HETEP is also the setting of the sun, the time of day when the peace of the evening spreads over the country. Then work is done and it is time to rest, a time for meditation and silence. Seated like a scribe before the table of offerings, the sage became HETEP—serene and peaceful.

Here is how "peace and love" is written in hieroglyphs:

HETEP	HENA	MEROOT
peace	*and*	*love*

If a man has lived his life correctly, he will reach the shore of the other world in peace (HETEP).

35 Hieroglyph for eternity

DYING IS BEING
PUT TO THE STAKE!

Death is expressed by this term:

$$\text{MET}$$

The word is composed of 𓄿, M, + ⌒, T = MET, determined by the figure of a collapsed man with blood running
from his head. A synonymous MET means "the vessel, the
conductive canal." For Egypt, physical death is likened to a
rupture in the vessel, an interruption in the circulation of
energy.

But this word "death" (MET) is linked to the word
"mother" (MOOT) in that for the just, death is not an end, but
an entrance into the immense body of the cosmic mother,
where resurrection occurs.

Here is another way of saying "to die":

$$\text{MENI}$$

The word is composed of ▭, the checkerboard, which is
read MEN; ∿, N (the same N from the preceding MEN that is

put there by the scribe to make reading easier); and ◊, I, = MENI, determined by ◊, the stake.

MENI means "to reach, to be fixed, durable." This navigational term means that the trip went off without a hitch and that the boat was correctly moored.

The term expresses the idea that a good death comes after a person has traveled through life, a trip that includes pain and joy and that finds a final point, a solid stake to which the sailor can tie his boat.

A LIVING DEATH

So we are dead and have had a good death. Where do we go, once Osiris has judged in our favor?

To a very specific place:

KHERET	NETER
underneath	*god*

𝌀 = KHERET, "the underneath"; ⌐ = NETER, "the god."

The sign of NETER enters into the 𝌀, to show that the divine has taken over this area. ⌒⌒ is the determinant, and shows that the necropolis is found in the desert.

This "underneath god" is the world of the dead, and of silence. Each night, the sun comes to visit and imbues it with the energy of rebirth.

The word "sarcophagus" is a Greek term meaning "eater of dead flesh"; it is an authentic mistranslation of the hieroglyphs:

NEB	ÂNKH
the master	*of life*
the owner	*of life*

The Egyptians thus show that the sarcophagus is not the site of death and shrouding, but in fact the area of regeneration (it is compared to a boat) where the process of rebirth takes place.

Similarly, rather than being the place of death, the tomb is

PER DJET

the dwelling place *of eternity*

DON'T TAKE THE BA OR KA AWAY!

Our vision of human beings is rather simplistic: a soul and a body and even, for many, just a body with a great machine, the brain. Although Egypt did not place man at the top of creation, it did consider him complex and endowed with a number of spiritual elements.

We have already mentioned the name (REN). There is also the

BA

soul, ability to move, capacity of sublimation

The BA is a beautiful bird; in human beings, it is the ability to move, to come out of the cadaver and tomb, to fly towards the sky, drink its energy, and come back to the mummy, which is the body of immortality. The BA appears as the mobile element of conscience, able to move in all worlds. To fetter and destroy it would be to condemn the being to "a second death," to emptiness. That is why several magical formulas are used to keep the BA from being taken away.

One must also preserve the

KA

the vital power

The KA is energy in a pure state. It is found everywhere—in stars, animals, plants, stones, and man. Eating is absorbing the KA of a food. In physical death, the KA is not affected; to live eternally, one must be united with one's KA .

The resurrection process is finished when one has been transformed into:

$$\text{🦢}$$

AKH

This bird is an ibis with brilliantly colored plumage. The word AKH not only means "being of light" and "luminous being," but also "being useful." The root AKH is used to form words such as "the divine eye," the "place of light," "the fertile earth," "the royal place," and "the secret place of the temple."

There is no more enviable condition than to become AKH and "return to the light" from which the just being has come.

A MENU FOR ETERNITY

The brave frog 🐸, small and unobtrusive on the bas-reliefs, is a symbol of eternity.

In the inscriptions, there are usually two ways of expressing eternity:

$$\text{⦅⊙⦆}$$

NEHEH
luminous eternity

with the presence of the sun, and

$$\text{𓊖}$$

DJET
cyclical eternity

with the presence of the great snake and of the earth (⊂⊃).

To reach a joyous eternity, one must be "fair of voice" and ◮♀, DI ÂNKH, "full of life."

Just in case, in order to be sure that nothing was lacking,

Karnak. Pharaoh with the traditional wig, and wearing the loincloth, is the very image of serenity.

it was good to have a menu engraved in one's tomb with the foods that would be desired on the other side written out:

KHA	M	T
a thousand	*as*	*bread*

= a thousand breads

KHA	M	HENQET
a thousand	*as*	*jugs of beer*

= a thousand jugs of beer

KHA	M	KHET	NEBET	NEFERET	OOÂBET
a thousand	*as*	*things*	*all*	*good*	*and pure*

= a thousand of all the good and pure things

Thus fed, the reborn will take his place among the

IKHEMOO	SEK

those who do not die

He or she will also know the stars surrounding the North Pole, like the dignitaries surrounding Pharaoh.

Exercise 6

Question 1: Which hieroglyph embodies serenity and peace?

Question 2: What is the difference between 𓄿 ⌒𓅓 and ﹏ 𓏏𓏛 ?

Question 3: Why did Egyptians marvel at the flight of this bird: 𓅭 ?

Question 4: Why is this wish, 𓃾 ☥, so important?

Answer 1: 𓊵 , HETEP, the offering table.

Answer 2: The first word, MET, simply means "to die." The second, MENI, means "to die while reaching the shore."

Answer 3: Because this bird, AKH, is used in the words "being of light," "being useful," and symbolizes the highest spiritual state.

Answer 4: Because it means "to be gifted with life."

APPENDIX

Saqqara, Tomb of Mererouka. Two hieroglyphs: the flagel-
lum on the left and the fan on the right. The first is linked to
the cult of Osiris, while the second is used to write the word
"shadow," one of the elements that continues after death.

A call to the living

Anyone planning to visit the magnificent tombs at Saqqara and Thebes should know the following text. It was often engraved on chapel walls, to be read by the living:

I	ÂNKHOO	TEPIOO	TA
O	*living*	*who are*	*on Earth*
SOOATY	SN	HER	IS · · · PEN
who	*pass*	*by*	*this* · · · *tomb*
SET	N.I	MOO	
pour	*for me*	*some water*	

Cairo Museum. Steles often represent a number of events or acts, as is the case here: the veneration of a god, an offering, and a hieroglyphic text. The table between the adorer and the Sun god is laden with eternally renewed foods.

Amon, Master of Karnak

This is a text that visitors to the great temples of Karnak and Luxor will find on the walls:

IMEN	RÂ	NEB	NESOOT	TAOOY
Amon	Ra	master	of the thrones	of the two earths

NETER	ÂA	KHENTY
god	great	at the head of

IPET	SOOT
she who chooses	he places (meaning Karnak)

A translation of the obelisk on the Place de la Concorde, in Paris

The obelisk[1] erected at the Place de la Concorde—23 meters (almost 76 feet) high, 227 tons—comes from the Temple of Luxor in Upper Egypt.

It used to be in front of the pylon, on the western side, and, with a second obelisk, which is still in its original place, marked the entrance to a sacred place.

We owe the obelisk's move to Paris to Jean François Champollion, who was in Egypt in 1829 when he learned that the British were thinking of buying a number of obelisks from Egypt's all-powerful ruler, Mehemet Ali. Champollion turned himself into a businessman and began negotiations. He saw the obelisks as inestimable master-pieces on the brink of destruction, and he wanted to save at least one of them. So he suggested having the monolith transported to Paris for 300,000 Fr. The erection of such a monument in the middle of the French capital would have the added advantage of granting one of Napoleon's wishes.

French and Egyptian authorities agreed to the project and to Champollion's condition that the man in charge of this operation be a practical-minded architect rather than a scientist.

In November 1829, as Champollion was leaving for

---

1. From the Greek word *obeliskos,* usually a monolithic, quadrangular, erect stone with a pointed head.

Saqqara, Tomb of Idout. A young gazelle on a leash follows a man holding lotus flowers. The depiction of such peace and harmony may well be the hieroglyphs' greatest achievement.

France, Mehemet Ali assured him that the obelisk would indeed make the journey to Paris.

Charles X, king of France, sent the Baron Taylor to Alexandria in 1830 to conclude the deal. Everything needed to be quickly settled, as the Franco-Egyptian relationship was on the verge of deteriorating. Once the money had been given to the Egyptians, an engineer, Jean-Baptiste Apollinaire Lebas (1797–1873), was put in charge of moving the obelisk.

A special ship, the *Luxor,* was built. It left Toulon, France, in April 1831 and started the trip back from Egypt in April 1833, arriving in Toulon 40 days later.

Yet although the obelisk arrived in Paris in 1833, it was not erected in the Place de la Concorde until October 25, 1836, before 200,000 onlookers. Lebas expected the worst until the very last minute, when an anonymous onlooker, who saw that the ropes were pulled to the breaking point, yelled "Wet them!" They were, and the obelisk's second birth took place—its needle profiled against the Parisian sky.

The obelisk is Paris' oldest monument. It was consecrated by Rameses II, which makes the "triumphant Pharaoh" Paris' oldest protector.

In the sacred language of the Egyptians, an obelisk is called TEKHEN, which means "protection, defense." The great stone needle is supposed to pierce the clouds and disperse any negative forces, visible or invisible, that hover about the temple.

The first obelisk, and the model for all that followed, was that of the sacred city of Heliopolis, "City of the Pillar" and spiritual center of ancient Egypt.

During the Old Kingdom, not long after the Great Pyramids were constructed, a Temple of the Obelisk was built in Abou-Gorah, north of Saqqara. The most famous obelisk was erected during the New Kingdom, in East Karnak. It is the tallest known, and is now found in Rome. Obelisks were usually built in pairs and were thought to guard temples with their magical powers. They were so renowned that some were brought to Europe as early as in antiquity. There are now obelisks in Rome (which holds the world's record with thirteen), Istanbul, New York, London, and Paris.

Each of the obelisk's four sides shows a scene engraved on the base of the pyramidion and three vertical columns of text. The pyramidion represents the original stone, which emerged from the primordial ocean on the world's first morning. It was covered in gold, which the Egyptians called "flesh of the gods."

The names of Rameses II are written inside "cartouches," long ovals closed by a bow that represent the universe over which Pharaoh exercises his control.

SIDE FACING THE CHAMPS-ÉLYSÉES

The pyramidion

The scene represents the Pharaoh offering wine to Amon, the hidden principal.

Words spoken by Amon-Ra, master of the thrones of the Two Earths (Egypt).

Words to speak: I give you all coherence.

Words to speak: I give you all breadth of heart.

Texts written above the king:

The accomplished god, master of the Two Earths, Ouser-Maat-Ra,[1] the son of Ra, the master of glorious apparitions,[2] Rameses, lover of Amon, who is endowed with life, like the divine Light (Ra), eternally.

Text commenting on the offering gesture:

To give the wine to Amon-Ra

Vertical text to the left when facing the obelisk:

(The) Horus[3]

The powerful bull[4] rich in power, a king made strong by his power, who victoriously seizes any foreign land.

The King of Upper and Lower Egypt, Ouser-Maat-Ra, chosen by Ra.

The son of Ra:

Rameses loved by Amon.

---

1. One of the names given to Rameses II, which can be translated as "the harmony of divine light is powerful."
2. What we render here as "glorious apparitions" can also be rendered as "manifestations," "crowns."
3. Each of the king's names is preceded by a ritual title: *(The) Horus,* which means the celestial falcon, protector of the monarchy, "the King of Upper and Lower Egypt," and so on.
4. And here "powerful" has the added nuance of "victorious power."

All foreign lands come to him, laden with their goods.

The King of Upper and Lower Egypt. Ouser-Maat-Ra, chosen by Ra.

The son of Ra, Rameses loved by Amon, may he live eternally.

Central vertical text when facing the obelisk:

(The) Horus:

Powerful bull, lover of Maat[1]:

The Two Queens[2]:

Egypt's protector, the one who seizes foreign lands

(The) golden Horus:

Rich in years and great triumphs

The King of Upper and Lower Egypt:

Ouser-Maat-Ra, prince of princes, seed of Atoum and forming with him a single being to shape his kingdom on earth, eternally, and to provide the temple of Amon with vital foods. This is how the son of Ra, Rameses loved by Amon, acted for him in ritual. May he live eternally.

Vertical text to the right, facing the obelisk:

(The) Horus:

Powerful bull, lover of Ra, the ruler, who has great fury and great power, the one who makes all lands tremble with his radiance.

The King of Upper and Lower Egypt, Ouser-Maat-Ra, chosen by Ra.

The son of Ra:

Rameses lover of Amon, Montou[3], son of Montou, who acts with his arms.

---

1. Maat is the cosmic harmony that exists outside of humanity, but without which no happiness is possible.
2. Meaning the two goddesses protecting Upper and Lower Egypt.
3. A Theban warrior god who gives Pharaoh his full capacity of victory over the enemy.

The King of Upper and Lower Egypt, Ouser-Maat-Ra, chosen by Ra.

The son of Ra, Rameses lover of Amon, endowed with life.

SIDE FACING THE FRENCH
CHAMBER OF DEPUTIES

The pyramidion

The scene represents Pharaoh offering fresh water to Amon.

Words to speak: I give you all breadth of heart. Amon-Ra is before him.

Texts written above the king:

The accomplished god, Ouser-Maat-Ra, chosen by Ra, son of Ra, Rameses loved by Amon, endowed with life, permanence, and power like the divine light (Ra).

Text commenting on the gesture of offering:

To give water to Amon-Ra
May he act ritually, endowed with life.

Vertical text on the right, when facing the obelisk:
(The) Horus:

Powerful bull, loved by Ra

The King of Upper and Lower Egypt, Ouser-Maat-Ra, chosen by Ra.

The son of Ra, Rameses loved by Amon, accomplished sovereign, valiant, vigilant in searching for that which is useful to the one who gave him life.

Your name will be firmly established, like the sky.

Your life span will he similar to that of Aton[1] in heaven.

The King of Upper and Lower Egypt, Ouser-Maat-Ra, chosen by Ra.

---

1. Aton was the king of Amarna, the capital built by the "heretic" Pharaoh, Akhenaton.

Central vertical text when facing the obelisk:

(The) Horus:

Powerful bull of great strength.

The King of Upper and Lower Egypt, Ouser-Maat-Ra, chosen by Ra, eldest son of the king of the gods. He made him appear on his earthly throne, to be the sole ruler, he who seizes all countries. He recognizes him as the one who takes care of him, to strengthen his exceptional residence for millions of years that he is building in Luxor. It is he who chose him millions of times.

And that is how he acts ritually, the son of Ra, Rameses loved by Amon, may he live eternally.

Vertical text to the left when facing the obelisk:

(The) Horus:

Powerful bull, lover of Maat

King of Upper and Lower Egypt, Ouser-Maat-Ra, chosen by Ra.

The son of Ra, Rameses lover of Amon, victorious king, symbol of divine light (Ra), he who cares for the Horus of the double luminous land (Horakhty), luminous seed, the legitimate[1] child, engendered by the king of the gods to make him the sole ruler, he who seizes the entire country.

The King of Upper and Lower Egypt, Ouser-Maat-Ra, chosen by Ra.

The son of Ra, Rameses loved by Amon, eternally.

SIDE FACING THE MADELEINE CHURCH

The pyramidion

The scene represents Pharaoh offering wine to Amon, the hidden principal.

---

1. There is a series of puns that identify the king with a "matrix" and with the "celestial eye."

Words spoken by Amon-Ra, king of the gods

Words to speak: I give you all life, all permanence, and all power.

Words to speak: I give you all coherence.

Text written above the king:

The master of the Two Earths, Ouser-Maat-Ra.

The ruler of apparitions in glory, Rameses loved by Amon, he who is endowed with life.

Vertical text on the left, facing the obelisk:

(The) Horus

Powerful bull of great victories, who fights, thanks to his power, king with the great war cries, master of fear whose strength dismantles any foreign land.

The King of Upper and Lower Egypt, Ouser-Maat-Ra, chosen by Ra.

The son of Ra, Rameses loved by Amon, loved when he appears like the one who is in Thebes[1] .

The King of Upper and Lower Egypt, Ouser-Maat-Ra, chosen by Ra.

The son of Ra, Rameses loved by Amon, endowed with life.

Central vertical text. when facing the obelisk:

(The) Horus:

Ra's powerful bull who tears the Asians to pieces.

The two sovereigns:

He who battles for eternity, the lion with mastery over his heart.

(The) golden Horus:

The one with the great victories over every foreign land.

The King of Upper and Lower Egypt:

Ouser-Maat-Ra, a bull settled on the border to strip any

---

1. A pun on the word OOAS, "dominating power," which is part of the word Thebes.

country that would run before him, as decreed by Amon, his ven-
erated father.

And thus Rameses, loved by Amon, son of Ra, acts in ritual.
May he live eternally.

Right vertical text, facing the obelisk:
(The) Horus:
Powerful bull with his great regenerating feasts, loved by the
Double Country, victorious king in combat, who seizes the Two
Earths, sovereign with a great kingship, like Atoum.

The King of Upper and Lower Egypt, Ouser-Maat-Ra, chosen
by Ra. The son of Ra, Rameses lover of Amon:

The powerful of every country lie beneath your sandals.

The King of Upper and Lower Egypt, Ouser-Maat-Ra, chosen
by Ra.

The son of Ra, Rameses loved by Amon, endowed with life.

SIDE FACING THE TUILERIES

The pyramidion

The scene depicts Pharaoh offering wine to Amon, the hidden principal.

Words spoken by Amon-Ra, king of the gods.

Words to speak: I give you all life, all permanency and all
power.

Words to speak: I give you all coherence.

Texts written above the king:

The accomplished god, master of the Two Earths, Ouser-
Maat-Ra.

The son of Ra, master of glorious apparitions, Rameses loved
by Amon.

The one who is endowed with life, like the divine light (Ra).

Text commenting on the offering gesture:

Presenting the offering of wine.
May he act ritually, endowed with life.

Vertical text to the right when facing the obelisk:
(The) Horus:
Powerful bull lover of Maat, a king loved as Atoum, sovereign and son of Amon, whose beauty carries eternity.
The King of Upper and Lower Egypt, Ouser-Maat-Ra, chosen by Ra.
The son of Ra, Rameses loved by Amon:
As long as the sky will last, your monuments will last. Your name will be stable like the sky.
The King of Upper and Lower Egypt, Ouser-Maat-Ra, chosen by Ra.
The son of Ra, Rameses loved by Amon, endowed with life.

Central vertical text, facing the obelisk:
(The) Horus:
Powerful bull who fights with his strength.
The Two Sovereigns: The one who overthrows anyone who would try to reach him and conquers the ends of the earth.
The golden Horus:
The one with the great aura, who has the mastery of strength.
The King of Upper and Lower Egypt:
Ouser-Maat-Ra, seed of a divine nature. It is he, Amon, master of the gods, who acts for the jubilation of the great temple and so that the Enneade[1] of the temple of the great god be joyful.
This is how the son of Ra, Rameses lover of Amon, acted in ritual.
May he live eternally.

Vertical text to the left, facing the obelisk:

---

1. The community of the nine creative powers.

(The) Horus:

Powerful bull, son of Amon, king with exceptional monuments, with great victories, eldest son of Ra, seated on his throne.

The King of Upper and Lower Egypt, Ouser-Maat-Ra, chosen by Ra.

The son of Ra, Rameses loved by Amon, he who exalts the temple of Amon like a country of light in the sky, in his great and superb monuments to eternity.

The King of Upper and Lower Egypt, Ouser-Maat-Ra, chosen by Ra.

The son of Ra, Rameses loved by Amon, endowed with life.

The essential act of ancient Egyptian cultural life is depicted at the top of the pyramid: it is the offering. Here we see offerings of wine, which brings divine rapture, and of water, which purifies.

The king's names are repeated many times, as an affirmation that the gods have endowed his immortal being with the most essential qualities: life, power, permanence, coherence, and breadth of heart.

The obelisk shows Pharaoh in his glory and as a bull, whose power is of cosmic origin and lets him triumph over all enemies. The obelisk celebrates the eternal victory of the Master of the Two Earths, Rameses, whose name is as durable as the sky.

The language forms
of the ancient Egyptians

In ancient Egypt, hieroglyphs were the sacred language. From the 1st Dynasty to the end of pharaonic Egypt, they were the language of the temple and were used by priests.

Besides this learned language, which required a lengthy apprenticeship, the Egyptians had a spoken language, which, with time, evolved further and further away from hieroglyphs. There was also a rapid written language called "hieratic," in which hieroglyphs were no longer discernible, for they had been distorted by the hands of the scribes. It was, in fact, a sort of stenography, and its study formed a specific branch of Egyptology. Yet another form of writing appeared during the 8th century B.C., known as "demotic." It was partly composed of distorted Greek letters. Later, during the 2nd century B.C., the Coptic language appeared. It used ancient Egyptian with a Greek alphabet that mixed consonants and vowels. Some Coptic words retained a nuance of hieroglyphic terms. It is thanks to this language, which is still used in some rites celebrated by the Coptic clergy in Egypt, a dissident branch of Christianity, that Champollion was able to decipher hieroglyphs.

Hieroglyphs themselves evolved, although their basic principles remained unchanged. What we call "Ancient Egyptian" was the language of the Old Kingdom (from the 1st to the 6th Dynasty, c. 3500 to 2475 B.C.) that was used in the pyramid texts.

Karnak. The falcon Horus, Pharaoh's protector, wears the double crown. He is the most extraordinary hieroglyphic interpretation of the creative eye.

"Middle Egyptian" or "Classical Egyptian" was the language of the Middle Kingdom (11th and 12th Dynasties). Most grammar books describe this language, and it is the one that Egyptologists learn first. The famous *Sinouhe's Tale*, for example, was written in Classical Egyptian.

"Neo-Egyptian" was the language of the New Kingdom (18th to 21st Dynasty). Although it exhibited some innovation in comparison with the classical language, there were no extreme changes. During later periods, especially the Ptolemaic period, priests invented a number of new hieroglyphs, but most of these have still not been deciphered. But the way in which the language functioned remained unchanged. The sacred language revealed to the Egyptians by Thot was thus in use for four millennia before being resuscitated by Champollion in 1822. Despite history, invasions, and the death of their civilization, the Egyptians were able to create an immortal language.

For further study

Egyptologists learn hieroglyphs thanks to two often re-edited books: Gustave Lefebvre, *Grammaire de l'Egyptien classique* (first edition, Cairo, 1940), and Alan H. Gardiner, *Egyptian Grammar: Being an Introduction to the Study of Hieroglyphics* (first edition, London, 1927).

Lefebvre's grammar is quite austere and tries to present the hieroglyphic language according to classical European grammar.

Gardiner's grammar goes about it differently: it tries to teach hieroglyphs little by little, with many examples and exercises, although, unfortunately, the answers are not included.

Many books, mostly in French, English, and German, have been published since World War II. One is Carl Buck's *Elementary Grammar of Classical Egyptian* (Leiden, 1952). They are all quite difficult and use a technical language, which would have been very disconcerting to the old Egyptian scribes. Since most books refer to Gardiner and Lefebvre, it is a good idea to consult them first.

Let's be realistic: it is not easy to learn hieroglyphs on one's own, although, of course, some have managed. But most will take classes, either in universities or privately either way, an enormous amount of work is involved.

Another book to look at for bibliographic information is Christian Jacq, *Initiation à l'égyptologie,* Editions de la Maison de Vie, 1993.

Index